M I N O R I T Y
R E P O R T

How African Americans and Hispanics Can Increase Their Test Scores

Harry E. Gunn
Jaswinder Singh

Scarecrow Education
Lanham, Maryland • Toronto • Oxford
2004

Published in the United States of America
by ScarecrowEducation
An imprint of The Rowman & Littlefield Publishing Group, Inc.
4501 Forbes Boulevard, Suite 200, Lanham, Maryland 20706
www.scarecroweducation.com

PO Box 317
Oxford
OX2 9RU, UK

British Library Cataloguing in Publication Information Available

Library of Congress Cataloging-in-Publication Data

Gunn, Harry E.
    Minority report : how African Americans and Hispanics can increase
their test scores / Harry E. Gunn, Jaswinder Singh.
        p. cm.
    Includes bibliographical references and index.
    ISBN 1-57886-077-6 (pbk. : alk. paper)
        1. Educational tests and measurements—Social aspects—United States.
2. Minority students—Rating of—United States. 3. Test bias—United
States. I. Singh, Jaswinder, 1958– II. Title.
LB3051 .G86 2004
371.26'01'3—dc22   2003018117

∞ ™ The paper used in this publication meets the minimum requirements of
American National Standard for Information Sciences—Permanence of
Paper for Printed Library Materials, ANSI/NISO Z39.48-1992.
Manufactured in the United States of America.

This book is dedicated to members of minorities who struggle hard to get ahead.

CONTENTS

FOREWORD

For the past ten years I have been teaching a course entitled "Home, School, and Community Relationships" at Valparaiso University. The central question that drives the course is, "How do we collaborate and create partnerships with parents, schools, and community agencies to meet the needs of our children?" I use that question because I know that we all carry within our heads visions of what we mean by "It takes a village to raise a child."

Drs. Gunn's and Singh's *Minority Report* is an imaginative, elegant, and inspiring document-essential reading for everyone who believes that it takes more than standardized tests to evaluate the complex growth and development of youngsters. The report is a wise and very informative account. It leaves us with a fresh awareness of what has to be taken into consideration in assessing youngsters and helping them excel and compete. To quote from William Ayer's book *To Teach: The Journey of a Teacher*,

> Tests are surrounded by rituals that underline their central importance. They are also shrouded in secrecy-and no one really knows who those folks are that developed the test, or how they figured out what's important to know. After all, standardized tests can't measure initiative, creativity, imagination, conceptual thinking, curiosity, effort, irony, judgment,

valuable disposition, and attributes. What they measure and count are isolated skills, specific facts and functions, the least interesting and least significant aspects of learning. And yet, it is hard not to assume that since this
is what "counts," this must be knowledge. Learning is not linear; it does
not occur as a straight line, gradually inclined, formally and incrementally
constructed. Learning is dynamic and explosive and a lot of it is informal;
much of it builds up over time and connects suddenly. Breaking the grip
of standardized tests requires in part exploding the myth of scientific ob-
jectivity that cloaks them. Teachers, parents, and youngsters need to know
exactly how the tests are made, who makes them and for what purpose,
and who wins and who loses among test takers. Standardized tests are
plagued with inherent and intractable problems. This helps explain the
army of lawyers and public relations people employed by the big companies to keep test sales moving. Standardized tests are culturally biased.
That is, they distort the performance of people who are culturally or lin-
guistically different, regardless of ability, intelligence, or achievement.

This book discusses the power of standardized tests in the lives of students and their families, teachers, and principals, and it argues that it
may be necessary to find some alternative, to look beyond standardized
tests, when assessing and evaluating student growth and development,
particularly for minorities. The authors ask us to think carefully and crit-
ically about the social, ethical, and emotional aspects of standardized
tests and how they affect youngsters, their families, and their teachers.
Authentic assessment must be continuous, and it must account for and
accommodate a broad range of dynamics, interest, and abilities in assessing growth and development.

Although written with a focus on minorities, everyone who reads this
book is likely to get something out of it. If September 11 taught us anything, it is that we no longer live in the kind of world we used to live in;
the face of our world can never be the same. Most people realize that
the requirements for citizenship in the twenty-first century are very different than in other generations. Our demographics structure, family
structure, cultural differences, and socioeconomic perspectives have
changed; they present many new challenges and issues that school districts today must overcome in educating tomorrow's children.

Drs. Gunn's and Singh's book is very timely. Look at our society and
how it has changed. We must change also. As Herb H. Zimiles argues in

"Progressive Education: Our Limits of Evaluation and the Developmental of Empowerment" (*Teacher's College Record*, 89[2], 1987, 203–207), standardized achievement test are problematic in part because of their "exaggerated importance, the false validity that is imputed to evaluation data, the aura of definitiveness that they cast (even when evaluators are modest in their claims), and the tangled web of comparisons and wrong inferences they invite." Zimiles believes that "since we accurately assess the main lines of school influence, we should instead direct our evaluation efforts to assessing the quality of the school environment. Because the environments children are exposed to provides a reasonable basis to 'estimate the quality of school impact.'" I may add that we should also look at the culture of the school and see if it creates collaborative partnerships strategies with home, schools, and communities.

—Dr. Jose Arredondo, adjunct assistant professor
and director of multicultural education
Department of Education, Valparaiso University,
Valparaiso, Indiana

PREFACE

Our American culture uses a variety of tests to "select" the appropriate path for each person. This selection often determines who goes to school, which school they attend, what school placement they receive, and which career they eventually pursue. Once in the job world, people often take additional tests to determine how suitable they are for a particular job (e.g., honesty tests and aptitude tests). Our passion for quantitatively differentiating human abilities and skills stems from the fact that these tests are expected to be objective and easily scored and analyzed by sophisticated computers. This process nearly eliminates human subjectivity, but problems arise when the tests are biased. A biased test can yield only biased results; hence the generalizations drawn from these test findings can be misleading and favor certain groups of individuals for specific jobs or academic levels.

The current American society is multicultural and multiracial. Historically, America has been predominantly a white-dominant society, though workers from the Far East and Africa were brought in long ago to build railroad systems and work as laborers on farms. Today, Americans continue to encourage skilled workers (e.g., nurses and physical therapists) and unskilled farm workers to migrate to the United States. After the taking over land from the Native Americans, the United States continued to remain a white man's land. The Native Americans and other minorities, such as African Americans and Hispanics, remained subservient to the white man even after the English colonies had become independent.

These minority groups, particularly African Americans, did not receive equal status, even on paper, until recent years. Racial discrimination, in reality, continues to pose problems today. Discrimination on the basis of race, color, nation of origin, creed, and class is now unlawful. Affirmative action and equal employment opportunity laws have further helped bring equality to various cultural groups in several ways. When African Americans were granted civil rights and civil liberties and were allowed to become part of mainstream America, it was perhaps expected that their integration into the American educational system and capitalistic world would be instantaneous. Nonetheless, this has proven not to be the case.

At first, it was logical to develop educational and psychological instruments that were suitable for the majority cultural group. Problems arose, however, when the cultural face of the society changed but the instruments used to measure individuals' skills and abilities did not. It was only recently that educationists and psychologists began to modify existing standardized tests to account for ethnic minorities.

Few minority members were at higher education professional positions in the early years of standardized testing, so minorities did not have much intellectual influence in the design of these tests. Since the face of the American society has been rapidly changing and such minority groups as Hispanics may outnumber whites in Texas, New York, California, and other states, test biases have become important. Ironically, however, direct influence on the design and construction of these tests remains in the hands of white individuals, as they play a dominant role in academics and in the field of education. The literature on test construction shows that only a few tests are specifically designed for such cultural groups as African Americans (e.g., the Black Intelligence Test of Cultural Homogeneity, or BITCH) and non-English-speaking Hispanics (e.g., the Leiter International Performance Scale and the Leiter Adult Intelligence Scale, or LAIS).

One might have expected cultural assimilation and indoctrination to help these minority groups compete with the majority groups, but that obviously has not happened. Certain minority groups (e.g., East Indians, Chinese, and Japanese) who come to study and work in the United States do not experience such severe problems in academics or in the job market. Interestingly, these individuals come from non-English-speaking countries and themselves have limited knowledge of English; they go through long periods of cultural integration and assimilation. Their children, born and raised in the United States, by and large do well in academics and in the job market despite the fact that they are first-generation Americans.

Why, then, do African Americans and Hispanics, who have lived here for generations and are culturally assimilated, not do as well on tests? African Americans and Hispanics take the same tests as new immigrant minorities, without the disadvantage of being unfamiliar with American language and culture. It is quite evident that factors other than knowledge of language and culture are at play, factors that adversely influence the test performance of African Americans and Hispanics. These points will be discussed at length in the book.

Tests almost always have built-in cultural biases, making them unfair to most minority groups. Those who do poorly as a result of that bias often experience low self-esteem and profound discouragement; they often give up. Worse, minority groups may lag behind not only in academics (in terms of high school-dropout rates) but also in the job market, which may result in high unemployment. Many individuals begin to depend upon the welfare system and develop a propensity for unfair means to prosperity. Their failure to compete with the majority promotes reverse racial feelings and a sense of learned helplessness. Scores, grade-point averages, and A, B, C, grades are the criteria used to judge a person's skills and abilities in a specific field, reducing a person's entire self to a few numbers or letters. By contrast, members of the white, middle-class cultural group are usually familiar with these tests and have relatively stronger test-taking skills. This group expects to do well and has every advantage. We wish there were such a thing as a culture-free test, but there isn't. As a result, African Americans and Hispanics do not get a fair opportunity to show their uniqueness and talents.

This book's goal is to help African American and Hispanic youth improve their test-taking skills so they can progress through school and through life with a sense of self-worth and purpose. Our program offers procedures for youngsters taking tests, helps parents learn how they can assist, and looks at different ways in which test examiners can approach test takers so that children can improve their performance.

We wrote this book to help African Americans and Hispanics overcome some of the difficulties they face taking tests. It is intended not only to acquaint them with some general factors that influence test performance (e.g., reducing test anxiety and displaying competence) but also to provide solutions for disparities in performance. The book is likely to help individuals of all age groups attending school or hunting for jobs in today's competitive market.

Herrnstein and Murray made in their book *The Bell Curve* an impressive and controversial suggestion pertaining to raising cognitive ability: "No one knows how to raise low IQ substantially on a national level. We need to look elsewhere for solution to the problem." This book begins where *The Bell Curve* left off. On the basis of data and experience working with African Americans and Hispanics, this book attempts to make concrete suggestions to help these minorities to overcome the wide gap separating their test performance from that of whites.

For the purpose of accuracy and ease of communication, the book defines whites, African Americans, and Hispanics as culturally distinct groups rather than people of different colors. In this book, the "whites" refer to groups of people whose forefathers migrated from various European and other Western countries and who have lived in the United States for several generations. "African Americans" refers to a culturally distinct group the members of which were brought to the United States as slaves from Africa and have lived in the country for many generations. "Hispanics" are members of a culturally distinct group of individuals who are immigrants from Mexico, South and Central America (i.e., have Latin descent) and have lived in the United States for many generations. There has been a continuous influx of this population into the United States. This is the fastest-growing minority in the country today.

It is our hope that the pages that follow will help these minorities to become more aware of test bias and equip them to deal with factors responsible for their low performance on psychological, educational, and other tests. It is also expected that whites, who remain a majority, will become more sensitive to minority bias on standardized tests.

This book provides guidance for test takers to sharpen their test-taking skills, which should boost test scores. This aspect of score enhancement is certainly helpful but is unlikely to provide a complete solution to the many issues raised in the book. Many other variables are directly or indirectly responsible for lowering the test scores of minorities; these variables must be addressed so suitable, long-term remedies can be found.

In this book we provide two methods to help minorities improve their test scores: direct and indirect. In chapter 7, for example, we indicate that teachers, parents, educators, and individuals who construct tests play a large role in determining test performance. This is an indirect approach that we anticipate will eventually affect the test scores of disadvantaged groups in many ways. We also propose the direct approach of providing steps that students or potential test takers can take to enhance their test scores. The final chapter of the book provides direct advice to students in dealing with the psychological aspects of test taking, such as "psyching up." In this chapter we also provide advice for different kinds of testing, including answering essay questions, a recent addition to some standardized tests (e.g., SAT). But this book is not simply intended to teach students or potential test takers from minority groups to follow a certain regimen to improve their test scores; it also addresses the larger issue of the role of culture, society, educators, policymakers, and academic communities on not only the future of children from minority groups but also society as a whole.

The book is organized so the first two chapters discuss how our society relies on the quantification of human behaviors and abilities to place individuals with appropriate skills and abilities within certain academic levels, institutions, and jobs. In chapter 3 we discuss how academic tests are created, so test takers can learn how to enhance their test scores. In chapters 4 and 5, we outline the general reasons why African Americans and Hispanics score lower than their white counterparts on standardized tests. Insight into these reasons can help us address the underlying causes and thus allow minority children to improve their performance on various tests. Some cultures, due to their sociocultural milieus, lean towards the development of right- or left-brain functional capacities. Roger Sperry's seminal research in the field of neuropsychology of the two hemispheres has taught us that the left and right brains specialize in mediating and modulating different human cognitive, emotional, and behavioral abilities. Many prenatal factors, such as proper nutrition, medical care, intrauterine drug exposure, and the mother's mental health, can negatively affect the growth of mental faculties of children. Chapter 6 discusses the functional specialization of the right and left brains and the relationship between their functional growth and culture, as well as the ways in which society as a whole, parents, and teachers can help in the development of a child's left- and right-brain functions. An optimum development of the left and right brains through methods such as adequate brain stimulation, enriched environment, nutrition, and adequate health care for both the mother and the child are likely to create a balanced growth in both the left and right brains.

As you read this book, you'll find a number of issues that are presented as causes of low test-taking skills. Resolving these issues will involve changes in society and some will involve changes in student skills through programs we suggest in each chapter. It is vital to identify both strong and weak skill levels so you know where to build, where to correct, and where to support. We hope you'll try our techniques and we think you'll find them both rewarding and fun.

ACKNOWLEDGMENTS

First and foremost, we would like to thank all our patients at Mid-America Psychological and Counseling Services in Merrillville, Indiana, for their valuable insights, which propelled us into writing this manuscript and motivated this project. Dr. R. S. Bhatti provided insights into cultural diversity issues. Dr. Alan DeWolfe gave meaning to the complexities of race/class issues. Drs. Rosemary Bowen and Patricia Jones, clinical psychologists, gave intellectual insights from the African American viewpoint. H. J. A. Ramoli MD, PhD, Robert Nyquist, MD, and Dojna Barr, MD, gave intellectual input.

To Dawn Josephson, of Cameo Publications, thanks for her timely reading and editing of this manuscript, and for your insightful comments. We are also very grateful to Educational Design Services for their assistance.

To the Lake County Division of Family and Children (LCDFC) staff, the Lake Superior Court, CASA, Merrilee Frey, director of the Lake County Domestic Relations Bureau and staff, and the Lake Circuit Court, thanks for working daily to preserve Indiana families and keeping our children safe. We would especially like to thank the Honorable Judge Lorenzo Arrendondo for his lucid discussions on the subject of minority affairs, and for all the work he does every day to improve the quality of life for low-income Indiana families. Our thanks go to Congressman Pete Visclosky for his work on critical legislation that has helped Indiana families over the years.

We are grateful to our dedicated staff at Mid-America Psychological and Counseling Services—Shelley Glenn, Marcy Ramirez, Dr. Alan De-Wolfe, Dr. Kalyani Gopal—and to our therapists Anna Arceo, Theresa Dennie, Richard Eiseman, Susan Steffey, and Ellen Wilkerson for their hard work and commitment to improving the lives of disadvantaged youth and families.

To our friends, Bob Bowen, Tom and Kathy Spencer, Dharini and Shank Balajee—your support is appreciated. Harjit Kaur, special thanks go to you for your faith. We are grateful to members of the Writers Expression Group of northwest Indiana for their encouragement and support.

Thanks to our families—Vi Gunn, Bill Gunn, Buddy Gunn, Shifali Singh, and Sidarth Singh—for their unconditional love and immense patience with our endless preoccupation with our work. Bill, Buddy, Shifali, and Sidarth have taught us the value of children's love. Vi Gunn's creativity, pragmatism, and unstinted faith in the value of this work kept us going. Dr. Kalyani Gopal provided constructive criticism throughout the research for data and the drafting of the manuscript and was instrumental in the writing of the epilogue.

We would also like to thank Suzanne Hanna Gunn and Sharon Gunn for computer support, and psychologist/attorney Bryan Welch for his valuable direction and support.

INTRODUCTION

> Poverty, race, ethnicity and immigration status are not in themselves determinative of student achievement. . . . [A]ll children can attain the substantive knowledge and master the skills. . . . [T]he city's at-risk children are capable of seizing the opportunity for a sound basic education if they are given sufficient resources.
>
> —Justice Leland DeGrasse,
> Supreme Court of the State of New York

Anyone who decides to write "a serious book" does so to convey some underlying philosophy. Our philosophy involves a number of beliefs:

- Current tests are generally unfair to minorities.
- Every person is unique. Successful education requires developing and nurturing that uniqueness.
- Test scores can rise if people are taught how to take tests successfully notwithstanding their socioeconomic, cultural, or educational backgrounds.
- People feel comfortable revealing their strengths and weaknesses only when the atmosphere is one of understanding and respect. For example, if a child feels uncomfortable with a test examiner, he or she is more likely to perform poorly on a test.

- Current standardized tests are unfair to minorities. In general, African Americans tend to score fifteen IQ points lower than other populations in current standardized tests.
- All people have the potential to achieve great things if given a fair chance.
- The wide discrepancy in test scores between white and black/ Hispanic children is the result of the differences in opportunities available to children of various cultures and classes. Studies show that the children of parents with higher income, higher socioeconomic status, and higher education are most likely to have higher test scores.
- Children need constant support from their home, community, and school environments to learn more, develop better goals, and become high achievers. Children of parents who are actively involved in their education perform better on tests.

When we look at the world today with these beliefs in mind, we uncover two constants: we have no truly "culture-free" tests, and current standardized tests are biased in favor of the white middle class.

A STARTLING DISCREPANCY: AFRICAN AMERICANS

A recent report published by the Illinois State Board of Education clearly identifies the wide discrepancy between the test scores of white and black children. Although the data indicate an overall improvement by black students in recent years, black students still lag behind their white counterparts. For example, in tests of third graders, white students had a success rate of 76.1 percent in reading, while black children had a success rate of only 34.0 percent. In mathematics, white students achieved a success rate of 87.5 percent, while black students achieved only 45.3 percent. Consider these other startling facts:

- Since 1988, the test score gap between white and black children has widened, as the performance of whites on reading and mathematics has risen while blacks' scores have slipped in reading and have leveled off in mathematics.

- While most research focuses on average scores, blacks lag far behind whites in the upper ranges of most test results. Depending on the test, whites are ten to twenty times more likely to score at the highest levels.
- Black kindergartners have substantially weaker mathematics, reading, and vocabulary skills than their white peers. Eliminating the differences existing before children enter first grade could close about half the gap between black twelfth graders and their white counterparts. Addressing other factors such as African American students' self-esteem and study habits could close the other half of that gap.
- Teachers and test facilitators tend to underestimate the intelligence of black students, contributing to the test-score gap.
- These gaps continue throughout the students' academic careers. According to a recent study of the student bodies of twenty-eight selective universities, almost three-quarters of white students scored at least 1200 out of a possible 1600 on their SATs, while just over one-quarter of black students surveyed in the same study performed at this level, a difference of 50 percent.

Finally, the National Review of Scholastic Achievement sponsored by the Clearinghouse on Higher Education found that academic differences among various races are profound. In mathematics Asian students outperform all other groups, whereas Caucasians outstrip all other groups in English, science, and social studies. African Americans lag far behind all other ethnic heritage groups in every area assessed. In some cases, the gap between the achievement of African Americans and that of other groups is more than alarming—it is greatly troubling.

A STARTLING DISCREPANCY: HISPANICS:

In reading, according to the 2000 National Assessment of Educational, among fourth graders 40 percent of whites scored at or above average level, as compared to 16 percent of Hispanics. Other results of that assessment are equally striking:

- Math: Only 10 percent of Hispanics achieved a high proficiency level, as compared to 35 percent of whites.
- Just 13 percent of Hispanics students get college educations.
- Hispanic children frequently do not begin schooling until they are at the mandatory age.
- More than 27 percent of Hispanics drop out-the highest rate of all culturally distinct groups in the country; further, its members are more likely than those of other culturally distinct groups to drop out due to peer pressure.
- Among Hispanics, 57 percent finish high school, and about 10 percent earn college degrees; in comparison, 89 percent of whites finish high school, and 30 percent earn college degrees.
- Only 16 percent of teachers in predominantly Hispanic schools are fully certified.
- According to the U.S. Department of Education, 36 percent of Hispanics live in families with incomes below the poverty line.
- Hispanics will represent more than one-quarter of school-age children by the year 2025, and these children are likely to be educationally and economically disadvantaged.
- Hispanic children are concentrated in high-poverty, largely racially isolated schools.
- By the age of nine, Hispanic children achieve at two grade levels below white children.
- Although first and second-generation Hispanic children outdo their parents with regard to achievement, third-generation Hispanic children fall into the outcome figures quoted above for Hispanic children.
- In 2000, the ARC Center Tri-State Student Achievement Study reported that when disadvantaged students were given enriched curricula for a period of two years (1998–2000) and low income levels, reading scores, mobility, and percentages of different racial groups were accounted for, Asians, blacks, and whites did statistically better than children without the enriched curricula. However, Hispanics performed the same; enriched curricula did not make a significant difference in their scores.

WHITES VERSUS MINORITIES: TEST BIAS, RACE, AND SOCIOECONOMIC FACTORS

What are the reasons for such a startling gap between whites and minorities in their performance on standardized tests? The gap could be due to the instruments used or to the influence of socioeconomic factors. Are our testing instruments designed to assess the actual abilities of children or their knowledge of the culture they live in?

Until 1965, African Americans were deprived of civil rights. Discrimination was widespread; an African American was not legally permitted to sit next to a white person on a public bus. Standardized tests designed in those years were geared to assess the abilities of white individuals. It was apparently not thought important to use these sophisticated tests for minorities, who were considered subservient to the majority population.

When the civil rights movement emerged, the focus was placed on equality and on integration of the various ethnic and racial groups. While much progress has been made since then, much more work needs to be done to overcome the over two-hundred-year-old stereotype of minorities and of norms of cultural and academic deprivation. Many aspects of the pre-1965 society remain unchanged—not least that today's black students must still take tests that were not designed for them in order to progress through school, attend college, or even get a job. A community that was not even used to taking standardized tests prior to 1965 now needs to do so, and the children must take them without any training or preparation from adult family members who have taken the tests themselves.

Over the years, many concerned educators have attempted to standardize tests in ways that eliminate bias; however, the bias is so embedded in tests that it is difficult to root out. Today, fewer than ten tests are used to assess the abilities and skills of African Americans and Hispanics. Why? Many people argue that most modern tests have questions and samples drawn from all ethnic populations and that therefore the results obtained from these tests can be generalized to all ethnic groups. The flaw in this argument is that although many of today's tests include all populations, they do not eliminate the disadvantages of African American and Hispanic children due to their lack of knowledge of the dominant white culture.

1

HOW WIDELY ARE TESTS USED IN AMERICAN SOCIETY?

A test is a systematic procedure for comparing the behavior of two or more persons.

—Lee Cronbach

Many people think testing is a minor, routine business. If you think about it, you probably don't even know how many people make a living giving tests, other than perhaps schoolteachers. In reality, a large population of professional psychologists makes a living giving tests. Psychologists also play a significant part in businesses, using standardized tests to assess employees in industries and organizations. When you understand how widely tests are used in our society, you'll realize the necessity of develop test-taking skills. Our society and our education are built on the quantification of behavior. Familiarity with the testing process will reduce test anxiety and should help with test performance.

One role of psychologists is to examine the factors that favor optimum outcomes within an organization. Another is to maintain efficiency and positive management/worker relationships. Nevertheless, it may surprise you to learn that testing is a multimillion-dollar industry.

Tests are used in every aspect of our life, including to:

- Determine individual's interests and aptitudes (interest test batteries and aptitude tests)

- Determine a person's Intelligence Quotient, popularly knows as IQ
- Enter prestigious academic institutions
- Qualify for scholarships and financial aid programs
- Qualify to attend a college (SAT scores)
- Qualify as to attend postgraduate work (LSAT, GRE, MCAT)
- Determine personal aptitude for higher office
- Assess personalities, attitudes, and prejudices
- Select individuals for police or military service
- Assess fitness for duty for state and federal service
- Recruit employees and managers for businesses
- Assess psychopathologies and personality disorders
- Assess an individual's propensity for dangerous behavior
- Diagnose mental illness
- Identify gifted children and determine academic placements
- Determine mental disabilities (learning disorders, alexia, dyslexia)
- Assess the compatibility between people
- Select fitness of a parent
- Assess the impact of child abuse
- Assess aptitude for the military, the FBI, sensitive positions
- Evaluate learning potentials (e.g., Learning Potential Assessment Device).

Are you surprised at the prevalence of tests? Did you know that even in sports, tests are now used? Many professional teams want to know whether players they are considering drafting possess various traits. Likewise, many employers want to know not only the emotional stability of their employees but also their sales or management abilities. Only through testing do they get the answers they need.

All these factors make testing an important part of life for everyone. With testing so widespread, imagine how many doors close for a child who performs poorly on just one test; the lives of many minority children change dramatically. For example, a low SAT score guarantees that prestigious institutions of higher learning will be inaccessible to them.

MINORITIES AND THE USES OF TESTS

- Testing is a multimillion dollar industry.
- Tests are used in every aspect of life, from determining IQ and academic standing to assessing mental illness and identifying character traits and career success.
- Test taking continues well into adulthood.
- One poor test score can dramatically alter a person's academic and career path.
- Excessive dependence on quantifiable scores eliminates the possibility of knowing the individual as a whole.
- Tests take a narrow view of human personality.
- No account is taken of abilities that tests are unable to measure.
- Factors critical for success in life, such as ambition, imagination, and social skills, are untested.
- Tests are designed to measure success as defined by what an individual can score on a specific test.
- The push to score high on tests leaves little room for creativity.
- Quantifiable tests promote rote memorization and mental rigidity.

2

WHAT ARE TESTS USED FOR?

Ability testing is being utilized to dehumanize, damage, and destroy black children and youth through improperly labeling and classifying them.

—Robert L. Williams

From the time a child enters school to the start of his or her career and throughout the person's adult life, tests play an important role. Most people, however, fail to notice the many testing situations that arise, primarily because the testing does not occur on a regular basis. These various test scores, though, dictate the direction a person's life will take. The lines that follow outline the need and usefulness of testing, which transcends ethnic groups and minority or majority groups—no one seems to escape being tested in modern American society. By knowing for what purpose tests are used, you'll be more aware of the various types of tests and how they can best be taken. Usage gives a clue as to test construction and allows you to know what to expect.

If you think we are overplaying the importance and prevalence of tests, take a moment to do some personal observation. In the previous section we revealed just how prevalent tests are. Now, think of all the instances you have encountered that involved tests. Make a list of the testing scenarios you come up with and then compare your list to the one that follows. As you review the many testing situations presented, think about the impact the results would have on a person's life. Imagine how, as a member of a minority group, these test results could change the course of your life or career, especially if these tests are insensitive to your culture or value system and thus carry an inherent bias.

How have any of the following test scores have affected your life?

EARLY LIFE TESTS

School Readiness Testing

If a child wishes to start school at an early age, or if a parent or educational professional questions a child's readiness to begin school, the results of a school readiness test are often the deciding factor.

In one recent example of this sort of testing, Tommy, a five-and-three-quarter-year-old boy, was most anxious to begin school. The youngest of four children, Tommy saw his siblings go to school every day, and he wanted to join them. As he put it, he wanted to be like "the big boys." However, because of his birth date, he needed individual testing to prove he was advanced enough emotionally and academically to be able to begin first grade. His parents made a testing appointment, and within a few days Tommy joined a dozen other children at a testing facility to prove his school readiness. Some of the tests were individual (i.e., one examiner, one child), and some were group tests. Tommy, to the surprise of all who knew him, "failed" the tests. The tests deemed him ready to begin kindergarten but not first grade.

Tommy's parents thought there must be an error, so they hired a private psychologist, who gave a different grouping of tests. Once again, Tommy failed to do well. But this psychologist took extra time with Tommy, and through extensive questioning he began to discover a very stressed little boy.

After interviewing Tommy's parents, the psychologist discovered that they had extremely high expectations of Tommy, calling him their "brightest child." Tommy's mother had also pointed out that once Tommy started attending school all day she would be able to go back to work. Tommy knew that his mother wanted to resume working, so he felt great pressure to do well.

Fortunately, Tommy now had an experienced psychologist, who looked at his school testing results and noticed that Tommy did not do well on group tests. The psychologist had a hunch that Tommy would feel more relaxed if he could talk directly to his examiner. When the psychologist talked at length to Tommy, the boy began to open up and finally revealed his stress. In a short while Tommy became more relaxed, and when retested he did very well. He was able to start school in first grade that fall.

As Tommy's case proves, sometimes test scores in and of themselves are not always accurate and sufficient criteria for decisions about a child's life.

Grade School Placement Testing

Each child learns at a different speed. Grade-school placement testing helps establish how quickly a child is learning and helps determine if a child is in an appropriate class. Such testing is important, because if a comparatively fast learner is in a class of slow-learning children, the fast learner will become bored and unproductive. Often in our clinical practice we hear of children being disruptive and unruly because of the lack of challenge in their course work.

School placement must fit the potential of each child. Whenever children feel that their family or teachers think they are "dull" or "stupid," they act dull and stupid. We have tested many children who have just given up. As one boy said to us, "My teacher thinks I'm dumb, so I guess I am. I just don't care anymore." When assessed correctly, such problems can be eliminated by grade-school placement testing.

Special Education Testing

Sometimes children have special learning needs, such as a child who has a learning disability or is otherwise mentally challenged. Special education testing can determine the unique educational needs of a particular child. It can uncover everything from language difficulties to weak areas of learning.

Reading is a common learning problem and usually requires special educational techniques. Often we encounter parents who tell us that their child is "lazy" when in reality the child is struggling with reading and comprehension of written materials. Some children learn at a slower rate; they need a specialized teaching pace consistent with their learning speed.

Mathematics and spelling are other areas in which a child may be learning disabled. "Learning disability" needs to be differentiated from being a "slow learner," in that children with learning disabilities have average or above-average IQ levels, whereas slow learners function at borderline levels of average intelligence or lower. Another goal of special education testing is to find the child's strengths and build on them.

For example, Bill, age fifteen, was a prime candidate for special education testing. Teachers identified Bill as a slow reader, but his tests showed that he had high reading comprehension. Testing also showed that he retained his knowledge. Bill was very likable, but people described him as shy and generally something of a loner. His verbal tests showed very low-average ability, and his grades dictated that he was a low-average student. After talking with Bill, however, we realized that he had a love for the outdoors. When we looked at his career plans, we discovered that he wanted to pursue a law degree. Given his grades and his focus on outdoor activities, it seemed unlikely that he would enjoy that career. Subsequently, we explored Bill's mindset further.

Bill had filled out a form stating that law was what he wanted to pursue, but he never said why. When questioned further, Bill revealed that he was very close to his father, who talked about nothing but law. "Lawyers get more respect than anyone," Bill's dad often said. "People don't push them around." Bill loved his dad and wanted to live out his dad's dreams, so he was going to do what his dad had been unable to do. Those who worked closely with Bill believed there had to be a better career for him. We used the next variety of testing to uncover Bill's true potential.

Child Development Testing

Since children develop at different speeds, we need tests to determine whether or not children are progressing properly and developing age appropriate skills. When used correctly, child development tests are an asset. They can alert us to concerns pertaining to a child's development, so parents and teachers can take steps to alleviate the problem.

A major problem with child development tests is that many parents tend to exaggerate, both negatively and positively, where their children are concerned. If a parent views his or her child as "dumb" or in some other negative way, the child will reflect that perception on the test. Likewise, the child who represents the family pride will often try to overachieve to meet expectations. It is in these instances that a trained test facilitator is necessary.

ADOLESCENCE TESTS

Intelligence Testing

Possibly the most controversial of the tests discussed in this chapter, intelligence tests, are used to determine how bright someone is, what society should expect from the individual, and how quickly the person will learn. The more valid of these tests are conducted on a one-on-one basis.

The problem is that intelligence tests assume a consistent background; if background information on a person is insufficient, there can be question as to the test's validity. We were once asked to retest a boy who had scored 79 on his IQ test—well below average. Though the boy seemed unusual, he certainly appeared to be brighter than that.

After talking to him, we determined that he was fearful of making mistakes. He rechecked all his test answers so compulsively that he eventually ran out of time, could not complete the test, and ultimately failed the item. We suggested that we make the test a game, to see how quickly he could complete it.

He smiled and "played the game." When he finished in record time, his IQ now tested at 121. What a difference a person's perception can make!

Achievement Testing

Often used with intelligence testing, achievement testing helps answer the question, "How efficient is the person's learning process?" If, for example, a person has a superior IQ but is far below average in ac-

complishments, something is out of kilter. There might be a learning disability, an emotional problem, or just a lack of effort. The advantage
of the achievement test is that it quickly reveals the person's weak areas.

It is important to note that a low score on an achievement test does
not mean a low IQ; it just means that achievement is progressing at a
below-average pace.

Vocational Testing

When someone feels confused about future career options, vocational
testing is the usual course of action. Most professionals recognize
the importance of selecting work that meets their personal needs.
Unfortunately, only about 30 percent of the population performs work
that they enjoy. This finding points to a sorry state of affairs, especially
since enjoying one's work is a major factor in sound mental health.

Picking the right career is very important, but people often do not
know what choice to make. When we explained this to Bill (mentioned
above), he finally admitted his confusion. "Yeah, I'd get bored being indoors all day," he said when questioned. "But what can I do?"

Bill then took a vocational test, which revealed some interesting data.
We learned that Bill needed much solitude in his work, and the test confirmed that he enjoyed being outdoors. He did not like great quantities
of reading, but he did like drawing. He definitely did not wish to pursue
a political career, and he did want to be independent in his work.
Clearly, a law career was not for him.

After reviewing the test data, Bill began looking into career options
that involved photography, graphic design, and other art-related fields.
While he would have to work indoors some of the time, he felt he could
go outdoors for photo shoots or other creative endeavors. With this new
focus, Bill felt much better about his future.

Not all vocational testing has such a positive outcome, though. Sometimes it produces negative results, as in the case of George. Throughout
high school, teachers and family pushed George to seek vocational
counseling, and he finally did. One of George's most prominent traits
was his inability to read well. George knew of his reading challenge but
had never regarded it as a major problem. He had always wanted to
work on cars, and his vocational testing showed he would be good for

such work. Since the vocational tests confirmed George's ability to be a mechanic and work with his hands, George never sought help for his reading deficit.

After high school George did find a few jobs working on cars, but he was never able to move up to more demanding work. He soon found that he had to read (and write) in order to present a bill and list the repair services he had performed. He also had problems reading directions on work orders and therefore had problems following procedures. As a result of his inability to read well, George's career floundered. His vocational test had failed to account for how important reading was to mechanical work.

High School Placement Testing

The purpose of high school placement testing is to place high school students according to their speed of learning. We have seen many teens who became very frustrated because they were in classes that moved so rapidly that they couldn't keep up. The real problem is that they became turned off to school completely, not just to the particular classes that moved too quickly for them.

High school placement testing usually involves a group-testing environment, which increases the likelihood that a test facilitator will miss key information about individual students. Additionally, people who are not "test wise" may produce an inaccurate result in a group setting.

College Placement Testing

Like high school placement testing, college placement testing strives to group students together academically. Unlike the high school version, though, college placement testing allows students to receive credit for certain skills, such as the ability to speak Spanish. As a result, the student will be allowed to take fewer courses in that particular area and focus on other, more specialized classes.

A coauthor of this book (Dr. Gunn) had such an experience. While it seemed unimportant at the time, the extra credit received for knowing

Spanish meant being able to devote more time to learning French. Years later, the knowledge of two languages made it easy to meet the foreign language requirement of Dr. Gunn's doctorate degree.

College Entrance Testing

Which college you attend can have a major impact upon your future career choice. As a result, various groups visit high schools to teach students how to be "test wise" so they can gain college admittance. With such pressure upon students, it is easy to understand how anxiety can build up to the point of near paralysis.

For example, we knew one student who did very well in high school but could not pass a college entrance exam. Each failed attempt produced an increase of tension and more severe failure. This student began to see himself as a chronic failure, with no hope for his future. To help him, we offered relaxation classes and taught him some test-taking techniques. The combination worked. He finally passed an entrance exam, began college classes, and did amazingly well. He soon had a fine career. Today, he frequently comments that had he not overcome his weak test-taking skills, none of his current options would have been available to him.

Special Interest Testing

It is unfortunate that a large segment of our population is fearful of testing. This fear often hinders a useful tool that could make lives better. For example, we worked with two students who were attending a junior college. Joanne came for help but refused all of the testing available to her. We offered her the best help we could without being able to assess her needs or progress. We encouraged her to try a different course of study, but she stayed in the same rut, with classes she did not really like. She went through her entire college experience taking classes that did not appeal to her, and her grades reflected that dissatisfaction.

On the other hand, Bill, Joanne's classmate, took some tests to see if he had an interest or talent in music, art, or some other specialized areas. He tested very high in art and decided to take a few art classes. He enjoyed them so much that he changed his major to pursue his new love. Upon Bill's graduation, a major advertising agency hired him as a graphic artist. Bill said he had never thought he had much talent as an artist, but he had known he liked to draw. His current career is rewarding to him, partly because he loves the work.

Joanne did ultimately find her interest—in music—but it was more difficult for her to pursue that career after graduating college with an unrelated degree. She ultimately went back to school in order to pursue a teaching career, and she finally became a music teacher. While her story has a happy ending, the time and energy she wasted during her first attempt at college was unfortunate. If she had only agreed to testing earlier, she could have started an enjoyable career years sooner.

ADULT TESTS

Disability Testing

Sometimes people have disabilities that can interfere with future work options, yet they are not aware of them. In these instances, an employer may require the employee to undergo disability testing.

As disability examiners, we have seen clients who were so anxious that they could not be open with their testing program. They felt they had to answer questions a certain way to ensure their employment. However, test administrators can detect false answers and may report that the person is hiding something, which ultimately looks deceitful. Once people learn that such tests are actually meant to help them, they may feel comfortable enough to respond honestly.

Morale Tests

Many employers now administer morale tests to find out what their employees think of their work situations. This is a great motive, since we all know that happy workers are better workers. We have done this sort of testing in various companies, and it has produced some surprising results.

One small company had great unrest among its employees. Right from the start the employees resisted the testing program. They were afraid that anyone who cited something negative might be labeled a "trouble maker" and be terminated. After building trust with the group, we found that the problem causing unrest was related to communication. There were persistent rumors that the firm was going to be sold to a competitor. One rumor indicated that two well-respected middle-management people were to be let go and that the employees' health insurance was to be limited.

Once the employees learned that such rumors were untrue, the testing process was very successful. The company became aware of the issues that concerned the employees, and the management team addressed those worries in order to create a more productive work environment.

Honesty Testing

When work environments contain valuables, such as jewelry, machinery, or large sums of money, honesty testing often comes into play. Such testing is also common for police officers, since they have power over people. Honesty tests have in the past been controversial and are not deemed useful in schools or in many job placement firms. Depending on the work setting, though, people still may have to take them.

Drug Attitude Testing

Employers use drug attitude testing to determine if an employee is likely to use drugs. The theory is that if someone has a positive attitude toward drug usage, he or she is more likely to use drugs. This type of testing is beyond the scope of this book.

Executive Testing

Company officials sometimes conclude that they need a specific personality type to fill a particular position. In such instances, testing is a quick approach to finding someone who is creative, sociable, highly organized, or possesses some other valuable attribute.

Recently a company executive approached us to help him find an employee who was innovative, organized, and able to work independently. One of the candidates we tested impressed us, but a previous employer did not give the candidate a positive recommendation. The previous employer complained that the job candidate had a bad habit of interrupting others. When we retested the candidate, the cause of such a discrepancy was clear. The job seeker was fine when relaxed, but when anxious he became a chatterbox. We gave the job candidate some test-taking counseling and helped him find ways to handle his anxiety and stress while on the job. The company executive did hire the job candidate, and to at this writing he has a fine work record.

Emotional Adjustment Testing

When we need to know how extensive a person's problems are, emotional adjustment testing usually provides the answer. These tests are beneficial because people often have different perceptions of what constitutes "severe," "mild," "average," etc-what is severe to one person can be mild to someone else. In addition, people often hide their problems in order to give the impression that they don't have any. Emotional adjustment tests not only find the problems but indicate their severity.

Sometimes the test may pick up something not previously suspected. A recent client revealed that he was making many mistakes at work and had some memory gaps. We suspected that he might have a brain disorder. The client's whole diagnostic picture was confused, so we gave him a battery of psychological tests. The results indicated a bipolar (or manic-depressive) disorder that was causing impulsive behavior and concentration problems.

One problem with these tests is that they are based primarily upon self-report. Recently we met a client, meticulous in her self-observations, who had been diagnosed as having severe depression and anxiety. Her self-esteem was reportedly low, and friends described her as very withdrawn. We asked her to describe herself to us and to provide a history of her behavior over the past eight years. Based on her positive response, we felt there was clear evidence that she had previously overstated her problems.

Marital Adjustment Testing

When problems develop in marital relationships, communication often dwindles and neither side agrees with what has taken place. Accusations fly back and forth, such as, "You yelled at me," and "Sure, but you did it first." Such a "he said, she said" approach is difficult to evaluate. A major question to uncover is, "What do they want?" Since people often do not know they need help, psychological testing can shed light on the underlying problem.

A word of caution—people must use such test results for the right reason. One couple insisted on taking a marriage adjustment test to find out who was "wrong." The husband insisted on the test so he could show his wife that he was "right." Ironically, the test results suggested that the wife was more adjusted. Enraged that the test did not come out the way he wanted, the husband left the office saying, "If I'm that wrong I shouldn't be with her." He subsequently filed for divorce. Looking back, maybe the test results were a good thing: they may have prevented future emotional pain.

Competency Testing

Courts and social workers sometimes request competence tests to determine if an individual is capable of handling his or her own affairs. Some people, especially older ones, lose their memory over time and therefore are not be able to organize themselves or conduct business normally. We once encountered an elderly lady who was so confused and forgetful that she paid one of her bills three times.

Competence testing can also reveal singular deficiencies. For example, sometimes a person's math skills are impaired, resulting in inability to handle money. Other people become disoriented with respect to time or location. Still other individuals go for drives in their car and then cannot remember their way home.

Tests to evaluate competence tell whether someone can function in an adequate manner. The results help doctors know when someone needs help or may pose a threat to themselves or others, such as when driving a car.

A NEVER-ENDING LIST

As can be seen, there is virtually no area of our lives where we do not encounter some sort of testing program. While we may not like the tests themselves, they are an aspect of our culture we must endure. The most constructive approach is to become familiar and comfortable with the idea of tests and to become a good "test taker." In the long run, this approach will likely prove extremely worthwhile for all parties involved.

TESTS: AN INTEGRAL PART OF AMERICAN LIFE

- Many people mistakenly downplay the importance of tests in everyday life.
- Early life tests include school readiness testing, grade placement testing, and special education testing.
- Adolescents take such tests as college entrance tests, vocational tests, and special interest tests.
- Even adults are regularly tested, as in honesty tests, morale tests, and competence tests.
- When you become familiar with the variety of tests and improve your test-taking skills, you score better and achieve more.

③

HOW TESTS ARE CREATED

Our lives begin to end the day we become silent about things that matter.

—Dr. Martin Luther King, Jr.

A test, for our purposes, is a measurement instrument that helps in quantifying a component of human behavior. It is a sample of behavior used to predict some event, so knowing how the test is created helps you to master the skill. The invention of testing is attributed to Francis Galton, whose approach was to examine and assess individual differences. From the era of Galton, Binet, and Munsterberg to present day, computerized and objective ways of conducting group testing have indicated advances in the field of psychological testing. The first version of the test known as the Binet-Simon scale was published in 1905; it was designed to assess subnormal individuals. By 1908 the test had undergone extensive revisions and expansion, and had introduced the term "mental age." The concept of mental age implies that a child who is twelve years old in chronological age may have only the abilities of a person five years old in chronological age. Another revision of this test took place in 1911. In 1916 L. M. Terman of Stanford University revised the Binet test in order to apply it to Americans; the new test came to be known as Stanford-Binet Intelligence Scale.

Group testing begun during World War I, when psychologists created the Army Alpha Test, which required reading ability; The Army Beta Test was designed for illiterate individuals. In 1939, prior to the entry of the United States into World War II, Stanford-Binet was revised again, when David Wechsler published the first version of a series of "Wechsler Scales" that measured IQ and achievement. To date these have been most widely used tests in the United States.

The idea of "testing" itself, however, was that of a psychologist named Alfred Binet, who tried to construct a way to assess the mental abilities of children in order to determine their academic placement. However, the testing "revolution" did not take place until after the Second World War, when the military decided that it needed a quick and objective method to evaluate new recruits in order to place them in appropriate jobs.

Today, American psychologists appear to have a passion for testing and quantifying everything, including human abilities. Numbers and purposive categories appeal to them, because they allow human skills and abilities to be quantified in an "objective" fashion. Broadly speaking, psychological and educational instruments used to measure human abilities are thought to be objective. That is, they require an individual to identify an answer that best applies to the question or to choose the right answer from an array of multiple choices given.

"Quantifiable" tests are considered objective because the examiner does not have the means to change the scores or to assess why an answer was given. In essence, an answer is either right or wrong—there is no in between. Educators and other professionals construct these tests by putting together pools of factors pertaining to subject matter. They then use complex sophisticated statistical techniques—a process called item analysis—to identify which of these items are critical to the skills or abilities in question. Out of four hundred items, for instance, only fifty may be considered relevant and be used to construct a particular test.

After selecting the most important items, the examiner tests how valid and reliable the test really is. "Valid" means that the test measures what it is supposed to measure. "Reliable" implies that the test scores will be consistent regardless of the test taker's background or other factors. In other words, a test is reliable when its results are consistent. These two characteristics (validity and reliability) are critical in establishing whether a test truly measures and assesses certain abilities.

Most objective tests are classified as "inventories." That is, these tests are standardized on a large number of individuals within certain age ranges and educational and economic backgrounds. Some tests even consider the test taker's geographical location. Standardization of tests may require them to be administered in a specified fashion regardless of the evaluator or the test taker.

Many of these standardized tests are processed by computer; examiners feed the responses into a computer in order to obtain the test results. By giving these tests to a large population chosen by a method known as "sampling," "norms" are developed, which later act as reference points. Examiners can cross-reference individual scores against the group or population on which the test was standardized.

Basically, then, a test is a sample of behavior that is supposed to allow us to make a prediction about an individual's performance in some activity. For example, to test memory, we might ask someone to repeat the following digits: 7, 3, 6, 8, 7, 7, 1, etc. The basic assumption is that the more digits are given orally and then repeated correctly, the better the person's memory. But is that a fair assumption for everyone?

We have found that air traffic controllers are very good at repeating numbers, perhaps because they do such tasks in their everyday job. Likewise, salespeople are often very good at remembering names. Asians, particularly Chinese and Indians, are traditionally considered good with numbers and mathematics generally. This implies that if we are familiar with something, we generally do better. This leads to the basic question of whether tests can be fair to minorities if they are based on tasks and information unfamiliar to them. After all, if you don't have a chance to become familiar with something, then you cannot fairly be tested on tasks related to that knowledge. Only when tests are created with no bias and become 100 percent culture-free will there be a level playing field for all test takers.

SUMMARY AND ANALYSES: PROCESS OF TEST CREATION

- Highly trained professionals construct tests.
- Test construction requires a long process of data collection and complex statistical manipulation.

- Each test has a specific purpose.
- All tests must fulfill the criteria of reliability and validity.
- Most objective tests involve questions and multiple-choice answers.
- Tests help in identifying a person's future career, academic placement, and achievement levels.
- Test constructors must take a greater effort to eliminate test bias.
- Most tests have inherent test bias despite concerted efforts to eliminate such bias.

4

WHY DO AFRICAN AMERICANS AND HISPANICS SCORE LOWER ON TESTS THAN THEIR WHITE COUNTERPARTS?

Education commences at the mother's knee, and every word spoken within the hearing of little children tends toward the formation of character.

—Hosea Ballou

Why do we need to know? Many variables help lower test scores and thereby reduce life opportunities. Poverty, poor schools, low quality of teachers, and many other variables discussed in this chapter indirectly act to lower test scores. Other factors, such as a lack of enriched environment and proper guidance can directly affect test performance. Knowing how test are created can help explain unknown factors and thereby reduce anxiety.

We have performed psychological testing for over thirty year on people in all age ranges, in all economic levels, and from all racial backgrounds. From our experience, we have identified a number of factors that impact a child's test performance. We leave it to the reader to conclude which ones apply to African Americans and Hispanics. We pose the following questions:

- Does hunger impair psychological functioning?
- Do neighborhoods affect test performances?

- Does poor funding for schools affect test performances?
- Do cultural values affect test performance?
- Does positive or negative role modeling affect test performance?
- Does the age of the mother affect test performance?
- Does an absence of an enriched environment affect test performance?
- Does the absence of informal teaching at home affect test performance?
- Does variety of experience affect test performances?
- Does time spent with the father help mental growth?
- Does it help test performance to have a well-educated father and mother?
- Does access to academic help really matter?
- Has it mattered that certain careers were closed to minorities?
- Does parental involvement affect test performance?
- Does child neglect/abuse affect a test performance?
- Does amount of communication with the child affect test performance?
- Does early childhood experience affect test performance?
- Does social exposure affect test performance?

Answers: All yes!

SOCIOECONOMIC FACTORS

Poverty and Economic Status

Abject poverty kills intellectual growth and incentive. Poverty is one of the most common causes of failure and despair. The first consequence of poverty is a feeling of discouragement. Such people often feel that nothing they try ever works out. People in poverty have few opportunities, simply because they lack money. Just think of how many more resources a wealthy child has available. We have all seen people who could produce wonderful art, music, or dance but never got the chance to get good instruction to develop their talents. We can only wonder how many great artists or performers we have lost because they lacked the money to develop their gifts.

Single-Parent Household

Two parents are better than one. Most of the early life education that children get comes from their parents. Parents are role models and confidence builders for their children. Parents help children develop morals, understand the difference between right and wrong, and learn what it takes to succeed in life. Low-income homes often need two working parents just to afford the basic necessities. Sometimes the stress of long and unusual work hours and lack of money cause the parents to separate. When that happens, children no longer have both parents in the house as stable role models, and they suffer from various emotional ailments, including low self-esteem, guilt over the breakup of parent, and loneliness.

Over the last few decades the number of single-parent homes has increased. The increase in the divorce rate has worsened the situation. In our experience working with minority groups, we have repeatedly found children being raised either by a single parent (usually the mother) or foster parents or grandparents, as either one parent is completely missing in the picture or the mother has a lifestyle that does not allow her to raise the child alone. This is particularly true for children who become wards of the state.

Even in relatively stable households, when a low-income family has a high number of children and a single parent, the environment can have a negative impact on the mental and emotional growth of the children. The absence of one parent, particularly the father, leaves a child with a sense of abandonment. The trauma of not having a father continues to haunt children for the rest of their lives. The absence of one parent completely eliminates the possibility of social, emotional, and intellectual input to the child at the level experienced when both parents continue to play significant roles.

An average minority family (African American and Hispanics) in the lower economic range has certain general characteristics. Let us start with where they grow up.

Neighborhoods

These children commonly live in poor housing areas that are segregated from predominantly white neighborhoods. Public schools in white neighborhoods generally receive the most state funding. That is where the tax base is. It is no secret that when a public school system or a neighborhood increases the number of African American children around 20 percent or more, white families start moving out, taking with them their tax dollars.

This geographical segregation leaves most African American and Hispanic children with limited choices. They attend poorly funded, unsafe schools. It is from this point onward that society begins to impose division and segregation. The ideals of equal opportunity to excel and achieve fade away, and the gaps between whites and minorities begin to emerge. If parents of minority children want to send them outside their geographical area to a reasonably good public school, they are required to pay. The other alternative is to send the child to a private school; how many poor families can afford to do that? Much has been made of the proposed school voucher system. The debate continues with regard to the pros and cons of the voucher system; studies are handicapped by the fact that not all parents who could have asked for the voucher program in the past have taken advantage of it.

Unsafe Environment

Many minority children also live in communities with a higher incidence of crime and drug-related activities. As a result, an average family is more worried about basic survival than about how to get the best education for their children. Children in such neighborhoods tend to learn more about guns and protecting themselves than about reading and writing. Sleep is punctuated by gunshots, screams, and cursing. Children get used to witnessing and hearing about crime.

This lifestyle becomes a routine, and the child eventually becomes insensitive to such words and phrases as "guns," "getting shot or killed or caught," "drive-by shooting," "gangs," "dope dealers," "carrying a gun," broken into," "stolen." This is where a vulnerable child gets pushed around. Phrases like these are commonly heard: ". . . jumped on—He threatened to kill me—He had a gun—He punched me first." This is where the child gets his first exposure to gang members. A weak child feels that if he is a member of a gang he will be safe. Gangs provide brotherhood and a sense of belonging that broken families do not. Under these circumstances academic excellence does not present itself as a feasible alternative.

It is hard for an unsafe child to concentrate on education and future goals. It is still unclear whether building segregated housing for minorities was a good idea. It is commonly heard from those who do not live there, "I don't want drive through this neighborhood; I don't want to get shot; I don't like to take that road because it goes through a bad neighborhood; That is a bad neighborhood." Many retailers outside these neighborhoods do not accept checks if they see the address from a "bad" neighborhood. Some people living in these neighborhoods begin to hide their addresses, knowing that where they live is not considered a "good neighborhood." Concerned mothers send their children to better schools by providing the address of a grandmother, aunt, or other relative who lives in that neighborhood. These children may live with their relatives during the week and return to their parents during the weekends.

Child Neglect and Abuse

It seems that poverty brings many evils with it. A mother who cannot afford decent childcare relies upon neighbors, boyfriend, or friends. Some of them abuse and neglect these children while the mother is at work. Physical and sexual child abuse is reported more often in these communities. The usual perpetrator is a person who is "trustworthy." Most well informed people now know the consequences of child abuse and neglect for the future emotional development of the child. Perhaps the most insidious and devastating is child emotional and sexual abuse within the extended family systems of uncles, cousins, and stepparents. In the ultimate analyses, the long-term damage to our country from such abuse are truly abysmal.

Teenage Mothers

Children who lacked love and care in their early years sometimes long for a child of their own who can give them that love. Early exposure to sexual activity, absence of an ideal role model, and lack of proper supervision leave children a great deal of time to spend with their peers. Children from poor neighborhoods rarely go on vacation. So what do they do during their summer vacations? The answer in most cases would be, "Hang out with my friends." Sometimes preteen and teenage girls are encouraged by older adolescents or adults to engage in sexual activity. This results in early, unwanted, and unplanned teenage pregnancies.

In one of our cases, a twelve-year-old became pregnant by a slightly older peer who used to come over to visit. The mother worked night shifts and as a single parent was unable to provide adequate supervision to the child. Unsupervised children in unstructured home environments are very vulnerable. When they come home from school these children are alone until a parent comes back from work. These latchkey hours are critical.

Foster Homes and Separation from Biological Parents

Many parents who are substance abusers lose their children to governmental agencies, who place these children in foster homes. Thus the early bond between the child and parent is lost. Some foster homes are good, and others are not. Sometimes it is like falling from the frying pan into the fire. These children are often moved from school to school, depending upon how many foster parents they go through. They are usually separated from siblings, so a set of normal learning experiences do not take place.

Drugs and Alcohol

It is well known that drug abuse is high among minorities. Children born with drugs or alcohol in their systems routinely show delayed development in all realms. They are likely to develop many disorders, including learning disabilities.

In drug-addicted households, a parent may be absent for several days and nights; the oldest child cooks, cleans, changes diapers, and watches over the younger siblings. These oldest children can be very punitive and overbearing. These children have long-term adjustment problems and are often referred to as "worrywarts."

Absent Father

Teenage pregnancies are connected to raising a child without a father—who is either very young, refuses to accept responsibility for his child, simply disappears, or ends all contact with the mother. Just as we need both hands to clap, a child needs both parents. Father's absence has been examined in many studies, and the negative impact on the development of the child has been well documented in case studies and examples.

Complacency and the Welfare System

Many young mothers who single-handedly try to raise their children end up becoming dependent on governmental assistance. The welfare system, which was designed to give a person or family a second chance, becomes a way of life. Mothers who have many children by uninvolved and unsupportive fathers stay dependent on the welfare system.

With the rising costs of health care, housing, clothing, food, and other basic necessities, single parents who determinedly try to get off welfare face a losing battle with the federal and state aid systems. These women, who are initially too proud to accept welfare, end up doing so because of their inability to meet their children's needs through their pay. Women who work in the low-end jobs tend to be denied health and other benefits that are readily provided to jobless mothers. Some give up, turn to welfare, and fall into the category of "welfare moms."

Long-term use of the welfare system leads a family to an economic dead end. It perpetuates poverty into the next generation. Girls who are raised in this environment continue to receive low-quality education at home and school, and they have little motivation to succeed in academics, especially if they are looking to become welfare moms themselves. One's physical attributes and ability to get a guy with a nice car and cool clothes become the markers of success.

Poor Nutrition

Children raised in poor neighborhoods by poor young teenage mothers are very likely to receive poor nutrition. Mothers who raise several children alone or have drug abuse problems fail to obtain proper prenatal care. We have seen many cases where mothers have left little children in the house by themselves with little food in the refrigerator. Time and time again we have spoken to the oldest child of a household and heard stories about foraging in garbage cans or going to a neighbor's house and asking for food. Sometimes, neighbors informally adopt such children and feed them.

Often these cases do not come to the attention of child protective services for a long time, as the oldest child covers for the missing parent. When this child grows up he or she is more worried about the next meal rather than education. In one of several such cases that we have seen a child who had been placed in a foster home was brought to our clinic immediately afterward; the foster family complained that he hoarded food in his school bag, suitcase, under the pillow and bed. Further examination revealed that the child had not received adequate food under the care of his mother, who was a substance abuser and had left the child home without food for days at a time.

Mediocre Pre- and Postnatal Care

Poor neighborhoods have crowded hospitals and family health centers. Young mothers do not receive proper prenatal care do not even know what resources are available to them. Most of them do not have health insurance. Governmental programs can only do so much to meet their needs. Poor heath care leads to health-related complications for children even before they are born; their chances of developing normally of being born full-term are compromised. Pre- and postnatal care is highly significant for the healthy growth of a child; it has a far-reaching influence on the health of the child's emotional, cognitive, and behavioral development.

Poor Family Support

We have repeatedly observed that these neighborhoods have very little in the way family support systems. The young mother either comes from a broken home or her relations with her parents are strained; either way, her own children are likely to be deprived of their grandparents' love and care. The family the mother comes from, if its situation is unfavorable, can extend only a limited amount of help. The father of the child is already gone, the grandmother has her own problems, and sisters or brothers are in the same quagmire that this young mother is. The result is that the children grow up in an emotionally distant environment where informal learning opportunities from significant others are limited. Thus they are denied learning experiences that otherwise could have stayed with them all their lives.

Children who find support in their homes, communities, and school environments learn more, develop better goals, and tend to become high achievers. Specifically, they learn how to prepare for tests. These are the ideals we all need to strive for, because when children succeed in their academic pursuits, they often succeed in career pursuits as well. Clearly, academic achievement has a far-reaching influence on a child's overall development and future possibilities. The more we as a society help our African American children to test better, the greater success our country will have as a whole.

Lack of Positive Role Models

African American children find role models in sports and the media—like Michael Jordan and Oprah Winfrey, role models who have touched many children's lives. But thousands of children are deprived of such positive role models within their own families. On the positive side, however, are grandparents who decide to raise their grandkids. We have talked to dozens of grandparents who have given up their golden years and plans of traveling and relaxing to take on a rowdy, hard-to-manage brood of children abandoned by their mother.

A boy usually looks up to his father, but what if the father figure is missing? A girl looks up to her mother, but what if her mother is a substance abuser? Such children have a hard time finding a good role model in a cohesive family network; the result is that they find someone on the street, maybe a drug dealer, or another person who has an antisocial personality. Many children at this age are led to commit crimes either because they are dared to and want to fit in, or because they don't know what the consequences are. They begin to see that money is the way out of this vicious poverty cycle; they lean toward making a quick buck rather than climbing the academic ladder, which to them seems a long shot.

Poor School Systems and Overworked Teachers

Good schoolteachers are critical in any child's development. Teachers
are often forced to become surrogate parents, counselors, or friends. As
a result, teacher burnout in low-income neighborhoods tends to be high,
and good teachers leave for less stressful jobs elsewhere, especially
more lucrative ones in private or suburban public schools. The demand
for teaching skills remains high, higher than the availability of good
teachers.

Even when schools and teachers try to provide children the education
they need, socioeconomic factors, emotional demands of home and family, and pressures of society overwhelm many academically inclined children. Children who showed great potential in their younger years are
often jobless years later; they can be seen sitting on the steps of their
homes, disillusioned and dejected.

Disillusionment

There is no doubt that many students have the drive and motivation
make it in the academic world despite poor conditions. Even those who
reach the professional level, however, often find that themselves unable
to transfer their school knowledge to the real working world—a skill
most white middle-class children have, due to their social-cultural environment, early exposure to real-world competitiveness, the higher level
of general acceptance they have encountered, and our society's passion for quantifying everything. Cultural and race differences then
come into play, and young minority men and women find themselves
drawn into the race game. Black, Asian, and Hispanic women are especially selected to play the roles of minorities in large corporations.

Lack of Confidence

People who do not feel confident in their abilities are afraid to risk failure and are likely instead to give up. When taking tests, children who
lack confidence will not guess an answer, because they perceive themselves as "dumb" and see no reason to bother trying.

Living in the Past

In the past, many occupations (such as corporate leadership positions) were closed to minority members, causing this group to seek careers that typically paid less or in which only a select few could achieve real success—such as professional sports. Today, there is no limit on a person's career goal, regardless of race—but the more education a child obtains, the more opportunities he or she will have in the future. So while sports are still worthwhile for minority children, word games have a place too.

Depression

Depression often causes low test scores, because it makes life appear bleak and meaningless. For children, depression comes from feeling rejected and stuck in poverty. Depressed children are typically either withdrawn or act out in school and home; the latter are generally labeled as disruptive or problematic children. Teachers, already overwhelmed by the number of students in their classroom, do not have the time or patience needed to help correct the child's behavior. Consequently, the child either frequently visits the principal's office or is repeatedly suspended from school. Many of these children do not receive adequate counseling or therapeutic intervention by professionals, due either to a lack of financial resources or an absence of awareness on the part of parents. It is not uncommon for such children to end up in special classes for the emotionally handicapped, although they may otherwise be intelligent. This reinforces the chain of poor self-esteem, learned helplessness, self-pity, and low self-worth.

Exposure to violence

Violence, including domestic violence, is relatively prevalent in low-income family areas and causes a sense of futility among children. The more futile life seems to a child, the more anxious he or she becomes and, as a result, the more afraid of anything unknown. This fear ultimately reduces the child's chance of future success.

In our own practice we have repeatedly seen that children directly or indirectly exposed to violence suffer from posttraumatic-stress disorder and other emotional conditions that impact on a child's growth and development negatively and persistently. Imagine, not a household where children are unworried about violence and have emotional energy to devote to creative activities, but a child who wakes up to a violent household to hear that someone has been shot or that a friend's father has been arrested for violent behavior or a gang shooting.

Such a child is primarily concerned about his or her own safety—and for that very reason gang members lure them in, promising them safety. Many children join these gangs, not completely understanding the consequences. They are soon involved in gang-related illicit activity, and instead of learning to score better on tests, which could open doors to opportunities, they begin to enjoy an exciting lifestyle where academics and careers are unimportant. These patterns are more applicable to African American and Hispanic neighborhoods than to the white suburbs.

Poor Drive and Motivation among Teachers

Teachers, like most of us, often look for work where the money is, and that means high-income markets. Typically, the less prepared and less competent teachers go where they can simply get a job, and that is in less well endowed schools. Such schools are generally in lower-income areas. Imagine a child being taught by a mediocre teacher. Mediocrity naturally breeds mediocrity. These teachers are unlikely to keep up with new knowledge, and their motivation is likely to be low, as they are poorly paid teachers in low-income minority neighborhoods. These teachers are likely to give up easily on their students, who are perhaps no better motivated to achieve anything in their lives. Such a teacher, who is perhaps the most significant influence on a child's life, fails to recognize this opportunity to act as a role model. Their classrooms are often overcrowded, and relationships between teacher and pupil remain distant. Thus one of the best opportunities for positive impact on a child's life is wasted.

Child's Poor Diet

When children have poor diets, they have less energy, are sick more often, and miss more days of school. Poverty greatly affects diet, as those with little money cannot afford food that is nutritionally sound. We have examined several cases where a department of family and children's services involves itself because parents failed to provide adequate nutrition to their children, for a variety of reasons. It may be addiction to alcohol or drugs, or neglect. Sometimes inadequate parental education leads to poor nutrition for the child. This is particularly true of young teenage mothers who have little or no knowledge of good child-rearing practices.

Poor Verbal Communication Skills

People in the lower-income bracket who work more than one job or have irregular work often do not take the time to communicate with their children. Either they must work so many hours just to pay the rent that there is little time to interact with their kids, or they are so depressed that they do not want to communicate with anyone, least of all their children. However, children who have regular interaction with their parents generally fare much better academically. Parental interaction not only helps children learn to communicate but also enriches their vocabulary and general fund of information.

For example, parents who have family time on a regular basis, have dinner together, and inquire how each member's day has been thereby foster cohesiveness and emotional bonds, and add to their children's learning experience. Informal teaching, such as asking children questions from general knowledge or engaging them in exciting and intellectually stimulating games, are as important as the formal learning experience that generally takes place at school. Imagine, instead, a household where both parents wake up for work so early in the morning that their children leave for school at the same time or even later, and where the children return from school only to stay by themselves for hours before the parents return from work, usually exhausted and stressed. This leaves little room for verbal communication or informal learning. This situation is worse when a single parent, who must make ends meet alone, is raising the child.

Test Anxiety

Anxiety, especially test anxiety, causes children to do poorly on tests. Children naturally want to do well at any task they undertake, but when test anxiety builds they begin to doubt their abilities and do not exert their full effort. Parents who play only minimal roles in teaching their children expect their children to perform well in school automatically. When the report card comes, all they care about is whether the child received acceptable grades or made it to the honor roll.

Parental expectations add to the anxiety of the child. In households where parents are not excessive in their expectations and stay involved in their child's school career, a certain amount of anxiety is reduced. Most children are afraid to show their report cards to their parents, because they feel that their parents are likely to judge them. A child who is deprived of many of the resources needed to do well on tests must now face the judgment of his parents, who perhaps give only minimal positive reinforcement when the child does well and usually punishes, by grounding or taking away material things, when the child does not. Parents are either ignorant about the psychological factors that contribute to child's test performance or fail to play an adequate parental role.

In our clinical practice, children are often brought to our attention who are doing poorly in school and both the parents and teachers are unable to understand the reasons behind this inadequate performance. It is not uncommon to discover that the child has average or above-average IQ but that high test anxiety either created by teachers or parents prevents them from performing well in school. Some children who feel inadequate and have low self-esteem tend to perform poorly even on tests that they were adequately prepared for. Most tests do not allow a second chance, so the child's state of mind on a given day and time determine his or her fate. Many parents and teachers transfer their own anxieties and worries to their children, driving up the level of anxiety during preparation period for a test. A tense testing environment becomes an additional source of anxiety for the child and hence a reason for poor performance.

Lack of Comprehension

Children from low-income families or families where there is little adult interaction do not have much experience with verbal directions. When children cannot understand what they are supposed to do, they quickly become confused and are likely to mark the wrong section or answers on a test. In our own clinical practice we have observed that children from low-income families with little time with adults develop only limited comprehension skills.

It is our experience that questions such as "What goes on the envelope before we mail things out?" remain unanswered or answered incorrectly even among preteen children. Answers to questions like these are part of informal education, which is usually supplied by an adult who spends time with the child. Similarly, when asked, "Why do people read newspapers instead of watching news on television?" most children of lower socioeconomic status and minorities cannot answer; their families spend more time watching television, as this perhaps is the least expensive form of entertainment.

Negative Expectations

When children hear feedback from adults regarding their performance, whether positive or negative, they meet those expectations. Tell a child that he or she is "dumb," and that is how the child will act. Likewise, tell a child that he or she is "smart," and the child will live up to that expectation as well. In the households where inexperienced single mothers raise children, they fail to recognize the importance of their comments on child's overall performance in school. It is not uncommon to observe that when there is more than one child in the family, which is usually the case, parents tend to compare children with each other and start an unhealthy competition. Children who are not doing so well in school become the target of ridicule, which further hurts their self-esteem. They begin to live up to their reputations, good or bad.

TEST-RELATED VARIABLES

Culture-Free Tests

Culture-free tests are also called culture-fair tests. These tests do not rely on knowledge of a specific group or heritage. The first culture-free test was developed by the U.S. military during World War II; it was called the Army Examination Beta Test. It was designed to screen soldiers for their intellectual abilities, including those for whom English was not their first language. The decades since have seen the development of other nonverbal IQ tests, such as the Leiter International Performance Scale—Revised. These tests are designed to circumvent language barriers. There are important culture-fair tests such as the Learning Potential Assessment Device (LPAD), Culture free self esteem inventories, and the Cattell Culture Fair Series. The Cattell scales are designed to evaluate intelligence independent of cultural bias, educational level, or verbal skill. Although studies have shown that culture-fair tests decrease test performance discrepancies between whites and minorities, there are no indications that they are able to predict success in school. Again, these minorities need to overcome cultural barriers to do well in school despite good scores on the above tests. An understanding of cultural differences is critical in getting accurate results.

We have tested low-income families for several years and have repeatedly found that disadvantaged people are not taught sound test-taking strategies. Additionally, test examiners are often unaware of approaches that might reach the disadvantaged. It is generally accepted that competition in today's world is unfair. In reality, all people have the potential to produce great things if given a fair chance. The premise of this book is that there is a clearly defined expectation that those who start from a disadvantaged position achieve, at a minimum, equal status with regard to achievement.

Racial Bias, Class Bias, and Testing

The questions that must be raised are whether the existing tests measure the actual abilities of children or their knowledge of mainstream white American culture. Hernstein and Murray, in The Bell Curve, acknowledge the presence of culturally loaded questions but assert that the tests are valid nonetheless. They propose that blacks do better on questions that appear to be biased than those that seemed to be neutral. Their argument is essentially that bias in tests does not affect test performance. Challengers of this argument have replied that tests might theoretically predict how well the African American test taker has assimilated white culture. However, in pragmatic terms, the real test lies in how well the person as adjusted within the dominant white culture.

WHY DO MINORITIES SCORE LOWER?

With regard to class bias, disparities in test scores within the African American population, particularly in tests like the SAT, can be partly attributed to the family income level. Direct and startling correlations have been documented with regard to the family income level and SAT scores. For example, data from the College Board of Education suggests that the higher the family income, the higher the SAT test scores. For example, a family with an income of $14,375 has a mean SAT range of 1500–1600, whereas a family with an income of five thousand dollars has a mean SAT range of 400–499.

Racially Sensitive Tests: Do They Remove the Test Bias?

In 1972, Robert L. Williams attempted to demonstrate that the difficulties faced by whites attempting to take standardized IQ tests designed for African Americans are similar to those faced by African Americans taking white-based tests, such as the SAT, which has come under considerable criticism for its heavy cultural bias toward mainstream white culture. Williams accordingly created the Black Intelligence Test of Cultural Homogeneity (BITCH). This test is based on vocabulary, terms, and expressions specific to black culture—for instance, "If a judge finds you holding wood [in California], what's the most he can give you?" The choices are: "a) indeterminate [life], b) a nickel, c) a dime, d) a year in county, e) $100.00" Another test designed to assess the intelligence of African Americans is the SOB test, based upon the same premise as BITCH. Earlier, in 1968, the Dove Counterbalance General Intelligence Test, or the Chitling Test, had been developed to evaluate whether blacks did better on tests based on the African American culture. It is accepted that on the above-mentioned tests, African Americans do far better than whites due to cultural loading.

Unfamiliarity with Test Materials

People in the higher income brackets can afford learning materials for their children. People from higher socioeconomic classes are more likely to get their child a computer, educational software, or tutoring during summer vacation, even when they do not need it. These children spend their summers learning activities such as art, crafts, and music.

These children's parents also travel more and go on vacation more, which in itself is a learning experience.

This kind of informal learning is limited in households of single mothers who survive on welfare. Even those with jobs can barely make ends meet, let alone buy educational material or take vacations. Children from these families spend their summers playing basketball or other games or aimlessly hanging out with friends in the neighborhoods. Since they have a lot of free time and very little supervision, they are more likely to spend time with the "wrong" crowd. Their families do not go to public libraries, due to time constraints or simple lack of interest. Middle-class families extensively use public libraries, and thus their children have more exposure to educational materials and Internet access available there. Children who grow up in households where reading and books are part of routine life get more exposure to educational material. They also receive adequate role modeling. Parents who are relatively well educated tend to make themselves available to help children with their problems.

Limited Test-Taking Experience

A new experience for a child generally produces a high level of anxiety. If a child who has not had to take tests suddenly must take one, he or she may let the "fear of the unknown" take over and perform poorly. Prior life experiences enhance our ability to do well in similar or related activities. Children of white middle-class families have access to various forms of test-taking opportunities. For example, most of these children can go on the Internet and find various sites to take tests. Their parents can afford to buy test-preparation material for tests like the SAT. Some hire expensive tutors to prepare their children for these tests. Some even invest more in helping their children acquire techniques to score well on tests than in helping them learn the material.

These parents begin to prepare their children for these tests quite early in life. Many children from these households qualify to take the SAT as early as in the sixth grade. Now imagine a child who has limited experience in test taking and limited access to the test materials. The results are certainly going to be more favorable in case of the child who had extensive test-taking experience. One of us (Singh) has daughter in sixth grade (at this writing) who qualified to take the SAT, scoring 810. Reviewing her test performance we discovered that she did not know that there was negative marking; she thought that she was compelled to answer all questions whether she knew the answer or not. Obviously, this was a useful learning experience for her; SAT scores do not matter much at this age. But think of a child who is ready to go to college, takes the SAT, and makes the same mistake.

Unfriendly Examiner

Few adults, especially test examiners, realize the impact they have on the children taking the tests. When a test examiner is unfriendly or not unresponsive, a child's test scores greatly suffer. This is a very serious handicap and one we will discuss at length later. When the relationship between the examinee and examiner is unfriendly and the environment in which the child is being examined is less than congenial, test performances are quite likely to be affected. A little pep talk by the examiner, putting the child at ease, can go a long way.

Fear of Asking Questions

Children who are routinely teased in school may develop a fear of speaking up or asking questions. This is a factor adults need to be aware of, because if a child is afraid to ask for clarification, he or she may answer test questions incorrectly when they otherwise would not have. In a crowded classroom, where children have limited opportunity to interact on a one-on-one basis with the teacher and consequently have a limited rapport with him or her, children are likely to be afraid to ask questions. Familiarity and a cordial relationship between the teacher and pupil give a child courage to ask questions, whether simple or complex.

Tendency to Give Impulsive Answers

Children who give impulsive answers may do some from nervousness or inability to concentrate. Understanding why children answer a certain way can help improve future test scores. Children who are nervous, do not want to be put on the spot in front of their peers, or hope to impress their teachers or peers tend to give impulsive answers, which are likely to be are incorrect.

SUMMARY

The reasons for poor test scores are varied, and many children may suffer from more than one. African American children typically get hit hardest with respect to life circumstances that lower test scores. Financial conditions, family circumstances, living conditions, and emotional factors affect a child's ability to perform well on tests. Adults play a vital role in a child's test-taking ability. Children from minority groups living under economic hardships have limited exposure to formal and informal learning experiences, which ultimately affect their test performance.

5

REASONS FOR LOW SCORES ON SPECIFIC TESTS

Books were my pass to personal freedom. I learned to read at age three, and soon discovered there was a whole world to conquer that went beyond our farm in Mississippi.

—Oprah Winfrey

If I know what's wrong, I can fix it! When someone lives in poverty, there's good news and bad news. The good news is that the person will most likely develop inner strength and a lot of self-reliance. The bad news is that the acquisition of "street smarts" is often accompanied by falling behind in academic performance due to weak verbal and reading skills. This process usually starts in the family even before school age. On the following pages we discuss why African Americans and Hispanics don't perform well in tests of verbal and language skills.

There are many reasons for the lowered achievement among minorities. This chapter lists some of the key reasons.

Limited Experience

Minority children have a much narrower range of experiences. Families with low income do not have a chance to travel, for example. Questions test questions about the population or geographical locations of countries or the number of states in United States are questions which middle-class white students are likely to score better on than their counterpart Hispanics or African American children.

Limited Exposure

Some test items ask about missing parts on boats—what if you have never seen a boat? There are tests that require the child to arrange a sequence of boating or rafting experiences. Middle-class white American children are likely to do better on these subtests than their counterparts African American and Hispanic children due to lack of prior experience. In contrast, African American and Hispanic children are likely to do better if the test were to ask them to arrange a situation where a gunman is being captured by the police, due to their exposure to such situations.

Home Environment

If your family consists of a number of children and only one parent, who will demonstrate to them the miracle of reading? In addition to formal reading, a child also learns from the informal experience of reading—for example, a parent looking out the car window and asking a child to read billboard signs. Middle-class families often eat in restaurants and exercise reading by reading menus with their children. This is less likely to happen among minorities, who either not aware of the idea of informal learning or fail to recognize its importance. Also, children with no prior exposure to such learning may not be interested in learning to read in an informal way, being already turned off by reading in a formal school setting. Further, parents also fail to reinforce and encourage or reward the child.

Most IQ tests have sections pertaining to word knowledge or vocabulary. There is a direct relationship between word knowledge and reading. A child's vocabulary is built not only by reading, however, but also by listening to adults and frequently asking the meaning of words that the child does not understand. Imagine the household where parents are not educated and have no time to teach children or find ways to help them learn. This child is likely to have an underdeveloped vocabulary compared to a counterpart who is encouraged to learn "big" words even if the parents do not know them themselves. They may teach the child to look up the meaning of the words in a dictionary or on the computer.

Children who grow up in households where older adults have limited vocabularies and frequently use slang in their conversation have little opportunity to acquire word knowledge. In contrast, a child who grows up in an environment where adults are educated and play word games (e.g., Scrabble) is likely to achieve better results on word knowledge tests. In addition, since vocabulary subtests are integral parts of most IQ test batteries and are highly correlated to a person's assigned IQ, he or she is like to score better than a child from a minority group.

Limited Time

A single parent who works hard all day often does not have the energy to engage children in conversation. Imagine households where the children spends most of the time either in front of the television or on the street while the parents are at work. This leaves little time for interaction between the child and the parent. In addition to learning from teachers, we all learn from our parents and significant others. Children who are separated from mothers or whose mothers do not talk with them have relatively poor vocabularies and communication skills and delayed speech and language development. Many standardized tests have items pertaining to these domains.

Limited Money

Handling money is a good way to learn math—but what if you never have much money to handle? Math is an integral part of life, and there are a number of tests that test the child's ability to engage in mental calculations. In our practice, we have observed that minority children can successfully engage in simple math (depending upon their age) but have difficulty in complex mental calculations and hence do poorly on these tests. An effect of the factors mentioned elsewhere in the book is that minority children are trained to think in a concrete fashion and thus have difficulty in abstract tasks. These children typically have a hard time carrying out such mental calculations as counting by threes, counting or repeating numbers backwards, carrying out parallel calculations (e.g., numbers and alphabets), or counting backward by sevens from a hundred. The result is quite obvious; they score poorly on these tests, which affect their overall scores. Since all children like money, money can be a powerful instrument in teaching children how to calculate mentally and concretely. If used by a parent or an adult in the family, the child gets sufficient exercise to learn to compute mentally, a powerful asset on a test.

Learning Programs and School Funds

When schools lack funds they often must cut back services. Remedial reading and math programs are often reduced or even lost. It is not uncommon for rich private schools to spend a great deal of money on reading and math programs to help newly admitted students who are behind in these areas. In contrast, schools in minority neighborhoods, struggling merely to survive, cannot afford this luxury. The result is that children do not get the extra help that they need not only to pass the grade but also to score well later on state-sponsored standardized tests. Children from relatively rich families who are deficient in these areas find ways to compensate for their weaknesses, but children from poor schools and families lag behind and are never given the same opportunity. Most standardized tests are geared to assess reading, math, and language components more rigorously than others. For example, SAT has a significant portion devoted to quantitative learning and language. Children who do not receive remedial learning do not perform well on these tests.

Poor Health Care

Minority children and their families have relatively little money to spend on medical health. Untreated high fevers may cause brain dysfunction, which often affects reading. Mothers from poor neighborhoods, particularly minorities, do not receive adequate pre- and post-natal care.

Additionally, many mothers in these communities have problems with substance abuse. Children with intrauterine exposure to drugs or alcohol show developmental delays and learning disabilities, specifically speech and language development. The mother's health is a significant influence on the health of a newborn child. It has been routinely noticed that children who are born with these disabilities do not receive adequate care and treatment. Thus a large number of children fail to achieve academic excellence or even make it to high school, and many of them fail to pass standardized tests. Sooner or later they drop out from school.

A significant proportion of children with intrauterine drug exposure are diagnosed with attention deficit/hyperactivity disorder later in life. These children, when neglected as they group up, typically are labeled "learning disabled," as they cannot focus on tasks and are unable to sit still, therefore cannot learn.

Limited Educational Material

People living in poverty usually have few learning tools, such as books, for two main reasons. Parents have higher priorities, such as putting the food on the table. Secondly, parents fail to use resources that are freely available in their communities, like local libraries or bookstores (where one can read the book in the sales area and return it to the shelf without purchasing it).

We have frequently asked parents if they use such resources to educate their children. The usual answers reflect lack of awareness, time, or transportation. These stores are typically located in white middle-class neighborhoods, so getting there becomes an issue. Further, their children, who have not be trained early to visit these stores and spend time in reading and listening or turning pages of books, do not enjoy doing so. In contrast, middle-class white parents and their children routinely spend time in these stores or public libraries, do research, go on the Internet to do homework, and flip through books without buying them. This divides children into two classes of students—those who are routinely exposed to educational material and those who are not.

Practical versus Abstract Mental Set

Most minority children are more practical than abstract. For example, a dog and cat are "things you play with," not abstractly classified as animals. Use is more important than concept to these children, because they have so little to use. Likewise, the sun and moon are similar because they give light. Typical tests require the subject to discern hidden similarities between two apparently different objects or situations (e.g., hurricane and volcano); most minority children have a hard time conceptualizing this similarity. A typical response may be that "hurricane" has something to do with wind and rain; "volcano" has something to do with fire. This contributes to poor performance on tests.

Limited Unstructured Learning Experience

A child's first school is at home, where he or she learns to relate with people, show emotional reactions, walk, and talk (verbal and nonverbal communication). The school, in turn, provides opportunities for structured learning, following a certain curriculum. The curriculum usually includes learning about the country's sociopolitical system, community living, scientific discoveries, milestones in the progress of humans on this planet, the history of science, and important personalities.

Schools, particularly in poor neighborhoods, have limited resources for field trips to aquariums, science and history museums, or for picnics. These excursions are as important as curriculum-based learning in the school building. Schools in wealthy neighborhoods, particularly private schools, have larger funds for such activities; children in these schools go on trips, camping and traveling, even outside the country. When asked about political leaders, distinguished people, or famous scientists, a child who has been to the places where they lived has knowledge of them not only from books but at first hand. Similarly, a child asked who painted the ceiling of the Sistine Chapel has an edge in answering the question if he or she has been there. Think of families who take their children to concerts and Shakespearean or Greek dramas. Such not only widens the children's worldviews but certainly equips them to answer questions about plays, characters, and writers in a test.

Limited Allowances

Most disadvantaged children are not given an allowance—another good way to learn arithmetic. They are told by their parents that they must learn to value money and how difficult it is to make money. This argument remains unproven in child's mind, as he or she has a minimal opportunity to manage and budget money, hence learning rudiments of economics and math. In contrast, children from middle-class white families receive allowances and learn to control their expenses either by writing out budgets or through mental calculation. Many preteens and teenagers even use computer programs to manage their small allowances; many clever parents encourage them to do so.

When children reach an age at which they are allowed to work part or full-time, they love to have their own money. That becomes a problem when the child begins to earn money specifically for things that his parent could not afford to buy him. His focus is upon attaining material goods (e.g., video games, brand-name shoes or clothes). He begins to enjoy economic independence at the expense of his studies. He is now more interested in the short-term goal of making a buck.

In contrast to this are children from middle-class white suburban families, who are more likely to focus on long-term rather than short-term goals, on academic goals or career. There is a higher high school dropout rate among African American and Hispanic minorities than among white middle-class students. More middle-class white students make it to college and attain higher degrees. Minority children begin to get into the rut of working for minimum-wage jobs, which restrict their personal and professional growth.

Lack of Confidence

Many disadvantaged children feel embarrassed when asked to read out loud. This argument is linked to their home environment and upbringing, where there is little emphasis on academics. Because of limited reading, writing, and language related experience, the child loses confidence. Lack of confidence and fear of failure, in turn, drive down self-esteem; the child tends to become withdrawn, afraid to be picked on by other students in the class. Children from middle-class or wealthy families are less likely to face this problem, having been regularly encouraged to stand up and face people. All this builds their confidence, and even children of otherwise mediocre gifts begin to perform better.

Limited Books of Interest

Disadvantaged children need books on topics that interest them. If they do not, it is unlikely that poor readers will develop interest in reading. Children who get reading material about subjects they do not like are not likely to want to read it. Reading itself becomes laborious and boring rather than fun. On the other hand, a child who likes football or basketball and is eager to learn more about these games, given material pertaining to them, finds that reading is no longer a chore. The child tries harder and may learn to read faster. It is important to identify children's interests and provide them with material that maintains their interest in reading and learning. In minority households, parents fail to recognize the importance of these aspects of leaning or simply do not have the means to procure such materials.

6

LEFT- VERSUS RIGHT-BRAIN-BASED LEARNING AND CULTURAL BIAS

THE BRAIN

From Pregnancy to Birth

Why is it important to study this variable? In this chapter, we'll discuss the role of both the left and right brains in acquiring verbal and non-verbal skills. We'll also explain how the development of these skills can be affected by a variety of factors. The brain-behavior relationship is one of the most vital relationships known to humans. Many of us speak, do, learn, act, and behave without being sufficiently aware of the existence of the brain, which mediates, modulates, and regulates human behavior in every sense of the word. While learning new experiences or skills we pay little attention to the existence of our brain. We fail to recognize the complex neuronal connections among millions of nerve cells and supporting glia cells responsible for an act as simple as picking up a pen from the desk. Things happen so automatically and naturally that in everyday life we are rarely mindful of the most sophisticated human organ nature gave us—the brain.

Take, for example, when a child is conceived. A small brain begins to form within the cranium. Imagine that this developing brain is receiving hurtful chemicals such as alcohol, illicit drugs, or nicotine. Many mothers from minority groups do not know—due either to poor health care or lack of education—that these chemicals will harm their unborn baby's brain. Hence when their children are born, they are likely to have cognitive or speech or general development-related problems.

Nutrition

Teenage mothers are particularly vulnerable in this regard. They are young, and most of their pregnancies are unwanted. These young mothers end up having children when they are still children themselves. They are known to hide their pregnancies from their parents for as long as they can and thus do not receive adequate health care. Limited in their knowledge and experience to start with, such prenatal care as they receive is delayed.

These mothers are likely to continue to smoke cigarettes or abuse drugs, if they have such habits, during the first trimester. Nutrition is one of the critical factors during pregnancy, especially to the overall development of the fetus, and particularly to the growth of the brain. The mother needs to be aware from the conception of the importance of eating nutritious food, as the developing child is also being fed.

Drug and Alcohol Exposure

In our clinical practice we come across teenage mothers and young adult mothers who become involved with Child Protective Services due to substance abuse or neglect of their child or children. Let us take the issue of substance abuse, when due to the mother's substance abuse the child is born with drug in his or her system. The hospital informs Child Protective Services, which then take over the child to be raised by a relative or unrelated foster family.

Imagine a child who has been drinking alcohol throughout the time that his mother had been carrying him. Imagine another child who was exposed to cocaine throughout his growth in his or her mother's body. Children who are born with fetal alcohol syndrome (FAS) typically demonstrate physical, facial, and bodily features characteristic of children born with alcohol in their systems. These children have low birth weight and in some cases are diagnosed with "failure to thrive." They also show developmental delays, including speech and language—

especially if born with cocaine in their system. These children are more than likely than others to become learning disabled when they begin schooling. It has been frequently observed that these children get sick more often then other children. They are more prone to ear and other infections. Children born with drugs in their systems also show behavioral problems. Separation from their biological mothers immediately after their birth makes them more likely to have emotional attachment problems later in life. One of the critical causes of attention deficit/ hyperactivity disorder, ADHD, is intrauterine drug exposure.

What do these drugs do to the child's brain in the mother's womb? The child becomes an alcoholic or cocaine addict before his or her birth. These children, when born, pose a challenge to their physicians: they have breathing problems, they are underweight, and their APGAR scores are poor; they go through withdrawal from alcohol or cocaine. Think of the negative effects of drug and alcohol abuse on adults: they have health problems and their memory is affected, apart from the socioeconomic consequences of drug abuse. Now we can imagine how these drugs might affect children during their first nine months of life. Learning disabilities and behavioral problems are quite common in these children.

THE FIRST SEVENTY-TWO MONTHS

There is an old saying that a child is born with a clean slate (a tabula rasa) and that adults and society write the script of life on that slate. The first seventy-two months, then, are critical to the development of the child in general, and of the brain in particular. Young minority mothers have little support from their families; in most cases one parent is missing and the grandmother herself may be on drugs or otherwise struggling with her own life and relationships. While most middle-class parents try to do everything right, young mothers from minority groups in poor neighborhoods do not. A mother from the minority group has a higher chance of producing an unhealthy and sick child than the white middle-class mother.

Even if the child's brain is well formed, it requires sensori-motor stimulation to develop and for multitudes of neuronal and synaptic connections to form. We have routinely observed that children of minority mothers do not receive adequate stimulation. All five sensory modalities must be stimulated for adequate and healthy growth of the child. Many mothers from minority groups are either unaware of the importance of these stimulating activities or do not have the means to provide them.

Let us start with auditory stimulation. The child hears and begins to recognize his mother's voice very early in his life, when he or she can barely hold his head in balance. He or she begins to recognize the smell, or hear the footsteps of, his or her mother at a very early stage of development. The child's brain is now ready to receive stimulation and grow. Music, singing to the child, and talking to the child, even if the child does not respond, are simple and easy methods to provide auditory stimulation. The child should be exposed to outdoor environments and even crowded shopping malls and carnivals. The child needs adequate visual stimulation; colorful, bright toys are useful. The child requires physical touch for his sensori-motor development. Massages and baths are simple, easy, and economical activities that can help the child's brain to grow. However, because many mothers from minority groups are single and child care in their neighborhoods is poor, their children do not receive adequate stimulation. They may have slow mental growth, compared to a child who receives all kinds of stimulation during the first few months and years of life.

In our clinical practice we have observed that the father is frequently either not in the picture or unknown. That itself cuts down half of the stimulation and care that the child would ordinarily receive. The single minority-group mother may have more than one child and may be working extremely hard to raise them. These young mothers are usually neglectful of their child or children. They want to continue to lead the life of a teenager—going out, drinking, or doing drugs, or simply "having fun." They struggle with their relationships with men and continue to have children by fathers who then absent themselves. Many of these mothers are charged with neglect or abuse, and their children are taken away from them. Thus during the early formative years, when the child's brain needs stimulation, care, and nurturing for its optimum growth, it does not receive it. The effect on the child's brain is obvious.

THE ROLE OF THE BRAIN IN SPEECH, LANGUAGE, AND COGNITION

The human brain is the most sophisticated instrument known to mankind; its sophistication lies in its complexity and flexibility. The brain is like a computer in many ways. Imagine buying the most expensive computer in a store and not having the operating manual. You will not get the maximum benefit from that computer. In the same way, the human brain does not begin to engage in complex cognitive processes, speech, or language-related tasks automatically. It needs training and education; it needs to learn from the environment. You must train your brain to acquire certain skills.

Speech is a good example. A child who cannot hear cannot learn to speak. Why? Because the child cannot be stimulated, and the speech areas in the brain are not able to acquire that function. This child may have adequate receptive-speech capacity but compromised expressive-speech ability. Thus the expressive-speech area, which lies in the left frontal lobe of the brain (also known as Broca's area), may remain understimulated or underdeveloped as compared to receptive brain area (Wernicke's area). A growing child's brain needs "software"—usually acquired from the environment—to learn to function adequately.

The more we put into the brain in terms of software (environmental simulation), the more we receive from it. The developed brain is nothing but a conglomeration of experiences. These experiences do not happen automatically; we must make them happen. The more the brain gains in terms of experience, the more efficiently it will work. Every decade adds to five to ten points to the human IQ, as part of the evolutionary process. The increase appears to stem from a direct relationship between the brain and environmental input, rises with every decade. In the absence of any scientific data proving structural brain differences between whites and minority groups, it is safe to conclude that it is environmental input that accounts for the difference in their test performance in later years.

THE TWO HALVES OF THE BRAIN AND LEARNING

A cursory glance at an exposed human brain instantly gives impressions that there are two equal halves of the brain, right and left. A bundle of nerve cells acts as a bridge between the two brains. The left brain controls the right side of the body, and the right brain controls the left side of the body. It is now established that the two halves of the brain perform specialized functions essential for human survival. The role of the right brain—sometimes called the "silent" brain—is not yet fully understood, except that creativity, art, and music are some its functions.

The left brain is the talking brain; the speech areas are situated in this side of the brain in most right-handed individuals. It is called the "analytical" brain, as it analyzes and engages in complex mental calculation. This is the brain that faces the test of life. Most scholastic curriculums are left-brain based, with their emphasis on word knowledge (vocabulary), information, comprehension, speech, reading, writing, and arithmetic. It is quite obvious that the measure of success in our society of a child is based upon the efficiency of the left brain. If a child fails to perform well in academics, it is the fault of inadequate or nonoptimal functioning of the left brain. Tests designed to measure human abilities and skills are left-brain based.

It is not yet possible to measure the functions of the right brain by any test. Nonetheless, many cultures have promoted creativity, art, or music. For example, the ancient Chinese, Greek, and Indian cultures were more interested in architecture, poetry, sculpture, and art than verbal skills. Music (rap or jazz) is one of the centers of African American culture. The sociocultural milieu supports this interest and provides positive reinforcement to those who excel in it. Moreover, since the expectations from minority students are low in terms of success in academics, it is likely that minorities culturally place more importance on creative activities, as way to get out of poverty. It is thus conceivable that minority groups, for cultural reasons, emphasize the right brain rather than the left.

Sociocultural factors, over a period of time, favor certain skills. For example, African Americans traditionally love sports. They like basketball and football. Michael Jordan and Magic Johnson are heroes of African American communities. During slavery, African Americans were limited as what they could do, but because of their natural interest in music, they were able to excel in that, and faced minimal social stigma. Similarly, because of their physical prowess and height they were able to excel in sports. Also since they saw no hope of competing with whites in academics, both sports and music perhaps became natural pastimes.

They began to sharpen skills in music and its appreciation, thought to be specific to the right brain. Extensive practice in sports led them to develop skilled-motor learning, which is the function of sensori-motor areas, such as the basal ganglia and cerebellum. Language, reading, writing, and arithmetic skills were less stimulated. Thus it is at least theoretically possible that cultures, cultural values, and sociopolitical atmosphere have impacts on brain-hemispheric specialization and the growth of human skills and abilities.

Hispanic culture, on the other hand, has rich cultural heritage. The culture promotes such human values as fatalism and destiny; Hispanic children are taught that their destiny is predetermined, that belief, rather than reasoning, is fundamental. Hispanic culture thus is not particularly geared toward reading, writing, language, or arithmetic skills. A child growing up in his milieu is likely to have relatively little worldly drive; his left brain is likely to receive less stimulation to develop skills that could help him to succeed in life, at least from material point of view.

The above discussion at least provides a theoretical frame of reference in regards to both African American and Hispanic cultural groups, who tend to use or sharpen the right side of the brain and underemphasize the left side, the functions of which tests are designed to measure.

7

HELP FROM PARENTS AND TEACHERS

It takes a village to raise a child.

—Hillary Clinton

HELP FROM PARENTS

Parents can tell but never teach, unless they practice what they preach.

—Arnold Glasow

Two powerful sources contribute to a child's success: parents and teachers. Parents usually know their children's strong and weak areas. Teachers love to see growth in their students and look for a wonderful support team. As psychologists, we have seen that many of the above factors hit minority children very hard. The result is lowered test scores. What can be done? We will focus on three areas for giving children the help they need. First, let's look at what parents can do. When the topic of parental involvement in education comes up, parents often show frustration. "I care about my kids, but what can I do? I'm not a teacher," they often say. Actually, there is a lot that parents can do, whether they have had teaching experience or not. Unfortunately, many parents do not realize how important they are to their children's future and take a back seat in their child's education.

Parents have a great impact on their children's education. More and more evidence shows that when one parent is missing from the household, the child's achievement goes down. In fact, the high school dropout rate is much higher when the father is not present in the house. Think of what it would be if both parents were generally unavailable! In our clinical practice, especially while working with minorities, the answers to questions regarding the child's father are "Well, he is not in the picture," or "Anthony has never known his father," or "Her father never calls and does not want to have much to do with Jose." It is not uncommon to find that the mother has five children and all are fathered by different individuals who are not in their respective child's life. Thus now the mother is single-handedly trying to raise all these children, and intellectual stimulation and training are the last things on her mind.

Although it is hard to change the society or individuals overnight, certain remedies can certainly be adopted. These single mothers can be involved in a state-sponsored parenting program where they learn the value of early childhood experiences and the importance of these experiences in a child's life. These single mothers should be taught to involve themselves in their children's growth. Boyfriends and stepfathers can be good substitutes for biological fathers. If that is not possible, the mother has no choice but to be more diligent in compensating for the absence of a father figure in her child's life.

Early life learning is extremely important for lifetime learning. There is truth to the adage, "Use it or lose it." We are not promoting a high-pressure classroom environment where the approach is "Push those kids so they can be ahead of all their classmates." Instead, the goal is to find out what a particular child likes and then encourage that behavior. Children are beautifully spontaneous and reactive, and their emotional reactions tell the adult what they like.

Our first two principles, then, are: early learning is very important, and parents are equally important. A child never says, "When I grow up I want to be a kid." As a parent, you are a role model, but only if you are available to your children. If your children see that learning can be fun, they are likely to want some of that fun too. If you show your children that learning something new can be useful, they will want to develop that skill.

Learning does not need to take place in a structured environment. Many parents fail to recognize the importance of early and informal learning. The child does not have to sit at one spot with a book, paper, or pencil; learning can be part of life. Children should not feel that it is being thrust upon them.

All parents, for example, go to the post office. A trip with your child to the post office can teach him so many things, and it can also be fun. The parent can talk to the child about how people mail things to other people, why stamps are placed on envelopes, and what happens to the mail once we drop it in the mailbox. We can also ask such questions as, What is a delivery person? What role does he or she play in delivering the mail? How is mail taken to other towns and even countries? How long does it take for the mail to arrive? How can people can send gifts to others by mail? Ask a child to give money to the clerk, receive the postal stamps, paste them on an envelope. These trips do not cost anything, and the child gets to spend quality time with her parent and learn in an informal way.

John, a family friend, had a habit of turning the lights off when he left a room. His young daughter asked him why he did that, and he gave her his reason. His daughter was only five at that time, but she remembered the explanation. A month later, as she was turning off lights, she saw one of the cords sparking. She informed her father, who immediately checked the cord and found a badly frayed wire. His daughter may well have prevented a serious accident. This episode points to some important factors about this family. First, there is obviously good communication between the child and her parents. This child felt important to her parents and knew she could go to them when she needed some information. In this case, the father proved that he trusts his daughter by first listening and then investigating the situation.

John, a very fine observer, often spoke about how his daughter seemed to show great pride. Her self-esteem increased daily, and she always showed a great interest in learning. In fact, she studied electricity, and for one of her classes she wrote an article on what she had learned. Confidence does wonders for children; self-esteem builds at an early age. During these formative years, children have a great connection to their parents. We know this because when children attempt some new activity, they often want their parents present. As self-esteem grows, children venture into new areas of competition and activity.

But what if parents have negative expectations for their child? In these cases, children feel negatively about themselves. They will tend to expect failure, and in the later stages of low self-esteem, they will call themselves names. "I am dumb," you will hear, or "I'm not a very smart person." Since the child feels unable to contend with important challenges, he will turn to spending time with other "losers." Someone who suffers from feelings of worthlessness easily and willingly follows others. Her suggestibility increases, and she begins to associate with other children with similar problems and issues. It is as if the person were pursuing a whole new set of goals. Children who once showed promise now display poor judgment. Those who deal with adolescents see self-destructive behavior constantly—a kind of self-hatred.

Negative expectations for a child are particularly harmful because children are so vulnerable. Young children have not had a variety of experiences that can produce a background of positive feelings. Then, too, young children have limited contact with anyone but their parents. That is one reason why their parents' attitude is vital. Children tend to believe that they themselves must be at fault, never the parents. A child with critical parents, the kind of people who find fault with everyone, will feel she must be lacking something. But it does not have to be that way, and we offer some suggestions.

Our first suggestion is an obvious one and yet one that is frequently violated, especially when someone is very angry. The parent feels angry and for whatever reason lashes back at his child by engaging in name-calling. "You act like a dumb ———," we have often heard after school conferences. Suddenly there are accusations that this child does not try hard. Then the child begins to see him in that negative light, acting "dumb" and losing interest in school.

Then we as parents may begin to feel guilt ridden for our negative comments. We want to make it up, so we now start giving extra praise. What does that do? Now the child believes that she must really be a "loser," because of all the phony praise. A piece of advice: When you make a mistake, admit it to your child—and don't overdo the praise.

Each Child Is Special

First, each parent must make an attempt to find something special about the child, or each child. Parents can do this by sitting by themselves and just thinking about the child. They may suddenly discover a multitude of positive characteristics in your child. These positive traits do not need to be outstanding in the eyes of the world, just to the parent. For example, one mother told us that she came up with a number of positives and none had anything to do with worldly success. "I like the way he says 'Mom,'" she reported. "I also like the way he smiles and the curl in his hair. To me he is a beauty." This approach conveys to the child that love is not conditional.

The second step is to share with your children your positive thoughts toward them. It is sad how many times children respond with surprise that a parent finds something good about them. At this point, some parents may ask, "How can praise possibly affect my child's attitude toward testing and school success?" Essentially, it boils down to confidence and a feeling of worthiness. When people lack confidence, they expect failure and tend to give up quickly. However, when people feel confident, they enjoy challenges, and learning brings pride of accomplishment. There will also be a greater desire to please others.

Next, take a good look at your child's more outstanding accomplishments. Discuss these with your child so she becomes aware of her talents. Remember the motto, "Everyone is special in some particular way."

Closely related to that is watching what is important to your child. We know a family where the son Jim was a great athlete, but he loved art much more. However, his parent usually praised him only for his athletic ability. They also believed he was not very good at art. Jim spent several years in school just drifting. Then a teacher discovered his artistic talent and helped him find interest in school again. Deep down, Jim had never wanted to invest much time in athletics but had felt that he had to do so to please his parents. Parents must place emphasis on things that are important to the child.

Talk and Question

Another important area is asking questions. Children must learn to ask questions when they need information. Never ridicule a child for asking what may seem like a "dumb" question. We have all at one time or another asked something that may not have made sense to someone else.

A friend recently gave a good example. Joe said that as a child he tended to ask a lot of questions. He described himself as open and very curious about everything. Unfortunately, Joe's father was busy most of the time, so Joe hated to go to him with questions. His mother also worked long hours and did not have time for questions. As a result, Joe often went to his teachers. One day Joe observed that the streets in front of his house were covered with ice. Two cars driving by nearly slid into each other. Joe went to bed that night fearing that the school bus would have trouble stopping in front of his house the next morning.

The next day Joe looked out the window and saw that the streets were clear of ice. How could that be? Joe thought to himself. The sun didn't come out at night, and the temperature had not been warmer. Joe wondered where the ice had gone. When the school day began, Joe's teacher asked if anyone had any questions. Joe immediately raised his hand.

"Can I ask a question that's not about the assignment?" Joe asked.

"Go ahead, Joe," his teacher responded. "It wouldn't seem like a school day if we didn't have one of your questions."

"Well, I was wondering how it gets warm in the middle of the night," Joe said.

Joe remembered that the children laughed, and his teacher looked dumbfounded. Had she simply inquired further, Joe would have explained his question better. The simple answer was that evaporation accounted for the loss of ice; melting need not have taken place.

One of our colleagues reported a similar occurrence at a higher educational level. Dr. Grims, a high school psychology teacher, had a student raise his hand and ask a question: "I know that schizophrenia means a 'split personality.' Does that mean there are two minds, and that each is half?"

Upon hearing the question, the whole class started laughing, and the student became very embarrassed. He didn't look as if he would ask another question for some time. Dr. Grims asked if everyone understood this question, and all answered they did. He then decided to try a different approach.

"If everyone knows the answer, I guess this is a good time for a test," Dr. Grims said. "Take out a piece of paper and explain the answer to our fellow classmate's question." As many would suspect, no one had the correct answer.

We want our children to ask questions, because so often their questions offer us a new way of looking at something. If we truly want creativity, we must be willing to travel a different path. Question asking clears up areas that are confusing to some students, and it often unleashes hidden creativity.

Parents and Learning

Another way for parents to help with the learning process is to get to know their children's behavior as related to the learning process. Parents are in a good position to make meaningful observations, because they are around their children so much.

A good question to ask is, "Is my child hyperactive?" This may be the case if a child cannot sit still, is impulsive, or makes careless decisions. Hyperactivity may also be present if there are concentration or memory problems. Perhaps your child cannot focus on any task for long periods of time. Sometimes there are learning disabilities, such as with reading or math. If this situation goes untreated, the learning process is likely to fall more and more behind grade placement. This will ultimately affect the child's self-concept and may finally cause a school dropout.

As much as possible, parents need to stay in touch with what is happening in school. It is a good idea to ask your child, in a casual manner, how things are going. This shows your child that you have an interest in his or her activities. For example, Teddy Benson found that he was falling more and more behind in school. He had particular trouble with tests, and he assumed that he was just a slow learner. "By the time I read the first ten questions, the time runs out," Teddy stated. "I just get started after the first ten minutes." Teddy was not truly hyperactive, just very anxious. His parents requested a school conference, and that led to testing. The results showed a reading learning disability. In time, they were able to correct the problem. These days there are ways of testing for attention deficit disorder, with or without hyperactivity. In some cases, medication provides a good solution.

Parents would do well also to take a good look at their own learning experiences. Some may have had an undiagnosed learning disorder. Parents may have understandable negative attitudes about school, and they may be unknowingly sending the wrong messages about learning to their children. We often find parents who have had academic challenges similar to those of their children. Heredity plays an important role in a child's learning. By knowing what a parent experienced, we can begin to diagnosis the child's problem. All this may help the child's future academic progress.

Get Involved

School conferences have much value as well. We have seen many conferences produce surprising facts. In one such conference, we spoke with teachers to learn about any particular problems they were encountering. A well-known teacher was the most talkative. Her name was Mrs. Lincoln, and she had taught in this school system for thirty years. She was well respected but also known to be aggressive in stating her opinions.

This occasion proved no exception. We started the session by asking if anyone had any questions, and Mrs. Lincoln immediately got to her feet. There was something about her besides her stature that commanded attention. She rose to her full height of six feet and squared her shoulders as if for battle. She was neatly dressed, and she gestured forcefully as she made her point. She had serious questions regarding the intelligence levels of the students she was to teach. For a number of years Mrs. Lincoln had been assigned classes in which the IQ scores were among the lowest. As a matter of fact, a year before this conference she had taught a third-grade class that had an average IQ of eight points lower than the next lowest class. Other students in the school mockingly called her class "the misfits" or "the dumb-dumbs." Other teachers openly sympathized with Mrs. Lincoln, but she had not responded.

The year of the conference, the school principal had asked Mrs. Lincoln to teach a class that was "gifted." The school leaders thought she would be pleased; the principal commented to various staff personnel how frustrating it must be to deal with "slow students" all the time.

At the end of the year, the school board calculated the achievement level of each class, and there were surprises. Mrs. Lincoln's former class showed a major drop in achievement scores. Mrs. Hughes, their new teacher, spoke of her frustration and admitted that she had lost her temper a few times. Other teachers spontaneously made comments about the slow pace of learning in most of the classes. For quite some time Mrs. Lincoln quietly sat in her chair, listening. Soon, however, she showed agitation, spoke up, and finally became engrossed in her feelings. She declared that children who were less bright were more fun to work with than the very bright ones.

"How could that be?" one of the teachers asked.

Mrs. Lincoln responded, "The real bright kids are snobs who always think they are better than the others. They want to challenge a teacher all the time, and all they think about is money. Some of them are spoiled and feel that everything should be done for them." For a few moments there was stunned silence. Then some of the teachers began to related their own observations. The conversation became very productive. The initial conclusion was that teachers, just like students, were not all alike in work preferences.

Mrs. Hughes liked the brighter students, and research showed that she did very well with them. Mrs. Lincoln, on the other hand, enjoyed the slower students and had great empathy with them. The children were able to sense which teachers had faith in them and which were more confident in their schooling. It was again the pattern of positive attitudes having a positive effect upon the children.

"So what do we do?" the school principal asked. "I have a school to run, and now I feel I'm being asked to match up teachers and students." Our recommendation was not to force any teacher to lead a class with which he or she could not identify. Teachers who were successful with slower children should be encouraged to teach such classes; those who preferred fast learners should be able to select that grouping.

Meaningful Interaction Promotes Success

We recall a story that one of our colleagues told about how when he was a child he had great fun with his dad. They didn't play with toys, nor was any major work involved. Instead, they used a little game to pass the time in the car as they waited for Mom to finish shopping.

Dad would start things off by pointing to someone about to walk by. "Okay, Son, what can you tell about this man with the dark jacket?" his dad would ask. The son learned to look at the man's posture, pace of walking, and general appearance in order to come up with an opinion—usually some wonderful observation.

"Well, Dad, he looks sloppy in his appearance, and his clothes don't seem well matched," the boy would offer.

"That's good son. Is he healthy?" Dad would ask.

Sometimes the son would answer that he didn't know, and Dad would come back with something like, "Well, how about his pace and posture? Is he sluggish or does he stoop over as he walks?"

The father and son enjoyed their time spent together. It made learning fun. Perhaps that is one reason why the son became a psychologist!

There is another approach that can be useful to parents. Often children do not see the connection between what they learn now and its future applications. We recall one young man who was convinced that he was going to be a pro football player. "Why should I have to study reading and writing?" he'd always ask.

We decided it might be helpful to have him watch a football game on TV and note how many former football players were involved with that game. He thought that watching the game was a fun idea, so he joined right in. He counted two announcers, four coaches, and one person who interviewed the players at halftime and at the end of the game. It was easy to point out that those were very good jobs, especially for former players too old to play the game. The young man began to study more diligently. When people see a point to something, they have more motivation to learn. Just like adults, children need a purpose in life.

A Jump-Start to Learning and Testing Success

We have written at length about the use of warm support and encouragement to make the learning process pleasant and successful. One final note: While we do recommend praise for your children, praise when it is not earned or called for misleads children, and they will at some point see its falseness. As we have warned above, they will conclude that they must be "dumb" for you to have made so much of so little. You must give praise on a reality basis, which will in turn build trust.

As you help your child improve his or her test-taking skills, realize that here as in most things, practice builds better performance. Merely taking tests over and over is likely to improve skills, provided it is not a traumatic experience—in which case it will just reinforce low self-esteem. Start with easy items and then gradually increase difficulty so your child senses progressive success. Positive reward is by far the most effective teaching tool.

Dealing with Failure

We have worked with a family whose philosophy was to prevent their two sons from failing in any way. They never allowed the boys to join an athletic team with other players were better than they were or that team lost more than it won. The family sought professional advice on how to pursue their goal but ignored us when we offered a different view. Years later these two boys both experienced failure and could not handle it. We believe that they had never learned how.

Parents should help children realize that failure is a great teacher. Remember Thomas Edison, who said he did not feel that he failed often—he had just "found eight hundred ways he could not make a light bulb work."

The principle is the same—don't let your child feel a failure because one test went the wrong way. That is an attitude that applies to any endeavor.

What's Going On around Me?

Many of the more widely used tests of learning potential have sections involving awareness of objects, or perhaps missing parts of objects. That may be unfair for children from families that have lower incomes. In one case, children were asked to name what was missing from an ordinary lead pencil. The correct answer was the eraser at the end. It must have seemed an easy question to the test designers, but very few low-income children got it. Eventually a brave boy said that in his class very few of the pencils had erasers; they had been worn away by usage. If you have not seen something, how can you recognize its absence?

It is obvious that relatively affluent people have more opportunity to have experiences (and form observations) than do those with lower incomes. But you can do wonders by using, for example, games while traveling in the car or even shopping in a grocery store. Such a game might be, "Show me a sign that is a rectangle, square, or triangle." The hunt may involve a color or even some part missing from a car. This type of game can be fun whole improving communication and at the same time making a child a better observer.

If your family travels, you can even use this approach to learn arithmetic. Supposing your trip will be one hundred miles and you have gone forty. What percentage of your trip have you covered? You can also set up a fun learning game with landmarks.

What Good Is Education?

Almost all parents tell their children that they need to stay in school. The teenager hears that until he gets sick of hearing it and may even become rebellious. Some families have been nearly pulled apart by this issue. Why the argument? The main reason is that the young boy or girl usually follows sports and reads about all the big salaries of so many nonacademic people. The teenager pays no attention to issues such as retirement (because that is too far away), or how few professional athletes actually achieve the top salaries compared to the numbers who compete for them and fail. He does not see that education helps people keep their jobs. It is the less educated who first lose their jobs. Further, where in the past, minority members were blocked from entering many fields even when they were well qualified, now there are more opportunities, and education has a real purpose.

Talk to your child about your educational background and what it meant in your life. If there is education that you did not get and now regret having missed, tell them that too. Let them learn from what you wish you had done. Being educated about the world of work is also useful. There are many interesting careers that are often neglected. If you as a parent can learn about these jobs and share that knowledge, you may provide another motivation to your young person to study more.

Young people in minority groups need to see that many members of their groups have become successful. This should give them motivation. Toward this goal there are many biographies on TV, in video rental stores, and available on loan or for a small fee at the library.

Aren't There Any Good Books?

Reading is a very important skill, and there is much that parents can do to help children become better readers. One approach that helps is to show interest in your child's progress. Ask your child, for example, to read a short article about sports, the weather, or travel. A second idea centers on knowing your child's interests. In our families there is great interest in dinosaurs; our children devoured anything they could find on the subject. In order to select good reading materials, however, you need to have an idea at what level your child is reading. If he or she is a slow reader in fourth grade, shop for books that are at the third-grade level. This builds confidence and proves that reading can be fun.

Frequently young people do not like the reading books that are used in school. If a student is a poor reader or, particularly, a slow one, interest may wax and wane. This is where the outside books become important, because they may be on more appealing topics.

Spend Quality Time with Your Children

People who have to work long and hard may just want to have a quiet evening at home. But if you can find time at dinner and perhaps after homework, it will greatly benefit your kids. Busy parents can also stay in touch with their children by calling them or leaving notes for them. Parent-child interaction is very important to education. It shows your children you take interest in them, and it improves communication by building vocabulary and other verbal skills. Research has shown that when communication is good there is a greater likelihood that children will mention their school problems, allowing them to be dealt with.

Sometimes one child is strong at, for example, reading, and another is good at math. Perhaps switch-off tutoring between them could be set up, with some reward system. This may help both children, because one's own learning improves when teaching others.

Additionally, children love riddles and other word games if they feel they are not being pushed. Examples: What is the difference? Between to, too, two: also? Know and no? What happens if we leap before we look? Parents can make up many more. The main thing is for the adult to show the child the ways in which tests can be fun.

Positive versus Negative Families

Leo Tolstoy said, "All happy families are happy in similar ways and all unhappy families are unhappy in their own unique ways." There are families that naturally have a positive atmosphere. Things are looked upon in a positive way; when a child makes a mistake, parents apply a corrective rather than punitive approach. Positive families obviously help the child to learn from their mistakes, and learning becomes a positive experience. Then there are families where the tone of the household is negative. In these families, parents consciously or subconsciously watch for their children to make a mistake so that they can pounce on the child and exercise their authority.

Autocratic versus Democratic Households

All functional and dysfunctional families develop environments that respectively encourages or discourages children to participate in making decisions, such as what to do over the weekend, how to entertain guests, or where to go on a family vacation. Some parents simply let the child know the decision made by the grownups; the child is completely left out of the decision-making process. Some other families sit around the dining table and encourage each family member to participate in dealing with a situation or issue. The first approach does not allow the child to learn how to develop inductive or deductive reasoning; the family fails to take an opportunity to become closer and more cohesive.

Let us take, for example, a family of a large number children whom a young mother is single-handedly trying to raise with limited governmental resources. This is not uncommon in both African American and Hispanic families. The mother's decisions are usually thrust upon the children. This does not help a child learn to make decisions; hence they are likely to grow up dependent and unable to make decisions for themselves. Now put this in a test-taking situation, where she is required to think independently, confidently to exercise mental flexibility to arrive at a decision. Training from her parents would have been handy.

Respecting Children and Their Viewpoints

Yes, a child is a child. A ten-year old is not expected to go out and make a living, and a child should not be expected to act like an adult. Many parents fail to acknowledge that a child's abstract thinking has yet to be fully developed. For that very reason, children should be listened to and their viewpoints acknowledged, no matter how wrong. Children should be encouraged by parents to express themselves freely; their opinions should not be cut down but corrected in a polite manner. This helps the child to express himself and ask questions of teachers or examiners if they are not clear about the nature of a test question. A child who is not comfortable in his seat while taking the test should have the courage to get up and ask for help instead of simply accepting what he has been given. Encouraging the child to ask questions and giving her viewpoint is very likely to have an effect on classroom and test-taking situations.

Think Like a Child and Act Like an Adult

It is also necessary to keep the child's age in mind while teaching a child. Parents like to lecture and give examples from their own lives as to how much worse their parents were and how they would have " taught you a lesson." These parents are wasting their time; their seven-year-olds do not pay attention to lectures. They do, however, pay attention when they are told something brief, even in a raised voice.

Children understand better when they are given instructions in a short, stepwise fashion. Parents must learn to think like a child and not expect their children to think the way they do themselves. The child's limited mental resources constrain the ways in which they can perceive life situations. The more we as parents adjust to the child's level, the better equipped we shall be to teach them and help them to grow emotionally.

In our clinical practice, parents have brought in their children with the primary complaint that they are not doing well in school and have behavioral problems. It is not uncommon to discover that it is not the child but the parents who need help—they are expecting the child to think and act like an adult. A parenting approach should be corrective but not punitive, positive and not negative. When a bright child begins to perform poorly in academics, the parent first must make every effort to determine the cause of it rather than simply "grounding" the child. Some parents think that the child's grades will automatically improve once the child is pushed adequately. Parents first must get to the bottom of it and learn more about their child. It is possible that the child is now hanging out with the "wrong" or "cool" crowd, people who call academically bright children "geeks" or "nerds"—and your child is trying to be "cool."

Act Bright, Not White

Accept that black intelligence is expressed differently than white intelligence. From the cultural standpoint, thinking should focus on effective problem solving in creative ways that enhance the black intellect. Blindly copying what works for one culture is not likely to work in the long run. The value of parental and teacher learning should focus on encouraging the child to express his intellect. He should be taught to take pride in his cultural heritage.

Minority immigrant parents often teach their children to develop skills to excel and compete with majority white students. These children are often taught to be proud of their cultural heritage rather than to be ashamed of it. They are usually taught that they are unique in being children of immigrant parents. These children derive inspiration from their parents' struggle as immigrants and often do well in academics and the job market.

Similar learning should be part of African Americans and Hispanic students. Their parents and teachers can use similar cultural-heritage arguments. Healthy competition is good; there is nothing wrong in teaching your child that he is unique and in no way inferior to any other culturally distinct group, including whites.

Setting the General Tone of the Household

Parents set the general tone of the household because they are there before the children come. Children simply join the existing norms of a family. It is up to the parents to decide whether they want to communicate in a polite or loud manner. It is they who determine whether cursing is allowed in the house or not. They determine what kind of games or toys are brought to the household, etc. It is parental communication that determines the quality and value of the relationships among family members.

Parents also determine the television programs, music, reading material, video games, communication, table manners, and content of discussions. The child is a latecomer. His brain is like a sponge and keeps absorbing everything around him. There is an old saying, "What you sow so shall you reap." The child is the product of his immediate environment—that is, his family. Thus parents must be cautious in setting the general tone of the entire household. Imagine a family where the child's parents are readers, bring home worthwhile books, take the child to libraries, bookstores, and educational concerts, and expose them to educational television programs (e.g., history, national geography, educational game shows) rather than sitcoms, which simply perpetuate mediocrity and indulge petty humor. In contrast, in minority families with limited resources and uneducated parents, reading material, if available at all, is of poor quality. The television shows may not be *Jeopardy* but lewd comedies that do not provide the intellectual input the child needs to succeed in life.

Summary:

- Parents have a great impact on their children's education.
- As a parent, you are a role model, but only if you are available to your children. If your children see that learning can be fun, they are more likely to want some of that fun too. If you show your children how learning something new can be useful, they will want to develop that skill too.
- A child will reflect the attitude his or her parent displays.
- Find something special about your child and then share that observation with him or her.
- Learn what's important to your child and what he or she enjoys. Encourage your child to develop that talent or skill.
- Stay involved in what is happening at your child's school. The more you show you care, the more your child will want to excel.
- Show your children that learning can be fun and useful to later life experiences.

- Give your child consistent and realistic praise to build his or her self-confidence, by describing some of your experiences.
- Talk with your child.
- Help your child not to fear setbacks.
- Find out your child's goals.
- Offer support during adversity.
- Seek professional help when needed.
- Develop communication for casual times (e.g., driving, dinner, etc.).
- Watch educational TV with your children.
- Help your child learn how to be sure what the teacher is asking; encourage questioning.
- Regularly ask about school.
- Be a good listener.
- Get to know those who evaluate your children. Are they qualified?

HELP FROM TEACHERS

> Setting an example is not the main means of influencing others, it is the only means.
>
> —Albert Einstein

At the very outset we must admit that teachers are probably the best chance minority children have to get out of poverty and a pattern of academic failure. They often work with children who have little family support and at times little respect for school. Those negative attitudes usually stem from years of failure and the resultant experience of humiliation by classmates and family.

Illustrating this predicament was our experience with a young student whom we had asked why his parents never came to school conferences. "I don't want them to, because all they ever see is how bad I'm doing." Think of the dilemma for that poor teacher! She recognized the student's academic problems, knew additional help was needed, but did not feel free to contact parents.

We must all realize that teachers have many demands placed upon their time and energy. Still, it seems legitimate to offer suggestions that perhaps will enable things to go better without adding yet more pressure.

We propose the following guidelines, which we prefer to call "rules," to achieve goals in terms of helping the child perform better on tests.

Rule 1: *Realize that all children want to learn.* We can safely conclude that if a child is not learning, something is blocking him or her and causing frustration.

Rule 2: *Make it fun.* We have always been disappointed to be told by students that school cannot be fun. In one of our teaching experiences a math teacher complained about her difficulties: "Anyone can teach psychology, because everyone finds psychology interesting, but few students find math fun." That sounded like a challenge, and we decided to test out our philosophy.

To do that we got a funny hat, a shopping bag, and cut out all the geometric figures we knew to exist. We placed them in the bag and then entered classrooms, where we were introduced as "funny clowns." Both of us responded by asking who could guess what was in the bag. As we had expected, the class was slow to respond. Then we offered support by saying we heard they were good guessers and knew "shapes." One daring girl was quick to respond: "Do you have a square in there?"

We looked in the bag and asked, "What color?" She immediately answered "Red." I took it out, and my partner held it up for the class to see. "Now help us empty the bag," my partner pleaded. The game was on!

Later the regular teacher told us they had never seen such a good performance, and she demonstrated the procedure to a group of first-grade teachers as an audience. "Everything was about the same except that the students guessed the trapezoid while the teachers did not," she said with a big smile.

Why is this so important to minority students? Because they often struggle in school and lose interest and motivation. They, like all of us, need recognition from others, and sometimes special games give them a chance.

Rule 3: *Make every effort to find the positive in each student and then reward it.* Post positives in the classroom and let the class know the special attributes of each. A child may not be good in math but may show good leadership qualities. Another child may be a poor reader but good in sports. Thus a teacher must look for something positive in a child and use that to help the child boost his self-esteem and self-worth.

Rule 4: *Try to get help from parents to support improvement in key areas.* Make sure that you as a teacher make an extra effort to engage parents, even the least motivated parents, in this venture. Regular with parents is difficult but can be of immense help if the parents are not an active participants in their child's academic success. Frequent notes that must be returned to you with the parent's signature are useful. Asking the child to get his parent's signature on work that the child did in school is another simple method to get the parent involved. Invite the parents to special occasions, such as their child's birthday celebration in the classroom.

Rule 5: *Explain the usefulness and value of education.* Many children grow up without realizing the purpose for and value of an education. Something so obvious to adults remains elusive to children. Perhaps only in later years do they come to understand the value of education for fighting poverty and getting ahead on the social ladder. It is the responsibility of parents and teachers combined to make these students gradually aware of the usefulness and value of education. Teachers can use themselves as examples, relating how (if this is the case) they had few resources but made it anyway. They can also use examples of people they know or great men who were not given anything on a silver platter but worked hard to succeed. For children who do not have positive role models at home, teachers can be a great substitute; a good teacher can change a child's whole life.

Rule 6: *Build on what is positive now.* It is always easy to find fault with someone, and students in their young years are more susceptible to trouble. Rules are guidelines to foster discipline and teach responsibility; rules should not take over the lives of the teacher-pupil relationship. Teachers should make every effort to focus on the positives rather than negatives. It is particularly true in case of minority students, who frequently get in trouble stemming from their home atmosphere, neglect, abuse, and lack of supervision. Teachers should focus on finding something positive in the child, nurturing it, and helping the child recognize it. Every effort should be made to avoid punishment; the punitive approach should be minimized in classrooms.

Rule 7: *When possible let students tutor one another.* Help minorities see that their peers care about them. Many private schools have "Reading Buddy" programs. In these programs children from higher grades are paired with pupils in lower grades. The older children read for the younger children. This not only helps to build positive big brother/sister relationships but also gives younger children positive role models.

Rule 8: *Congratulate yourself.* As a teacher, you should be proud of yourself. Teaching is a noble profession. Imagine every year how many students are influenced by a teacher to be "somebody." There is nothing wrong in taking the credit for shaping the lives of young minds. Teachers leave ineradicable memories in their grade-school students, good or bad. These memories live with them forever. We have heard phrases like, "I owe to my grade school teacher for my success," or, "My grade school teacher was so bad and hurt my self-esteem so badly that I simply gave up." Most teachers try to play their roles to the best of their ability and knowledge. Such teachers should be congratulated for being a main line of defense against the chronic failure of those who most need help and have the fewest resources.

8

HELP FROM EXAMINERS

Education is not the filling of a pail, but the lighting of a fire.

—William Butler Yeats

Just because you give exams to those trying to get ahead doesn't mean you can't help them. Use a little humor or a joke or two, and lighten up the session. You as examiners will feel better, too!

When conflicts arise between the child and the examiner, the child is not always wrong and the examiner is not always right. In fact, the first question to ask is whether the examiner feels comfortable with minority students and has some understanding of their various cultures. Since most tests are built around the white, middle-class lifestyles and values, examiners are likely to be more familiar with that culture. We need examiners who are sensitive to the various groups they will be working with.

MAKING THE EXPERIENCE PRODUCTIVE

Examiners, like parents, play a big role in a child's test-taking success. Below are some characteristics examiners should possess in order to make every child's test-taking experience more productive.

Ensures Fairness

The first objective is to make sure the examiner feels that he or she can readily communicate with minority students, particularly those from the lower income levels. Does the examiner enjoy working with minority groups? Has the examiner had ample experience testing this group? Can the examiner see individual differences between members of this group?

While there are individual differences among people in the lower income groups, when being tested they will all tend to be less verbal. They generally will not challenge the examiner as often, and they often will not raise questions even when they are unsure of answers. They will not guess very often, and they will be less prone to say they do not understand something. Some examiners resent conversation, while others prefer it.

One important thing to consider is what expectations does the examiner have. Do they start with the preconception that a particular group can be stereotyped as, for example, not bright? If they do, many students will behave accordingly.

Has a Sense of Humor

A good sense of humor is vital when dealing with any group that is different from the average; humor is a great tool for dealing with anxiety and breaking the ice. For example, we once asked a little girl, "Who was the president of the United States during the Gulf War?" She repeatedly said, "I don't know," and she refused to guess. We decided to take a chance with a joke, so we asked, "Well, was it Michael Jordan?" She laughingly responded, "No, silly! It was George Bush!" This use of humor was just what she needed to relax and be willing to take a risk. Talking out feelings of anxiety helps greatly and shows children that they are important.

Finds the Cause of Anxiety

Many children live in a constant state of anxiety, especially in regard to school matters. In order to correct this, examiners need to know the cause. Are the parents putting pressure on the child? If so, talking to the parents may help change some of their approaches to interacting with their children. The anxiety-ridden child needs support, not more pressure.

Recognizes Societal Bias

While our society has made some significant gains, racial prejudice still exists. African Americans and Hispanics have been the primary group hurt by prejudice, and those of a low income level have been hit especially hard. This constant negative message is likely to have a destructive impact upon children's confidence. The examiner can help by directly talking about the problem and by pointing out the wonderful contributions African Americans and Hispanics, or low-income earners, have made to society. It is important to remind them that much of America's success had been due to the achievements of members of different cultures.

Administers the Right Tests

Most tests are not standardized for low-income children. An examiner should use his or her technical knowledge to put together a program that is as balanced as possible. For example, years ago we were asked to do a testing program that would attempt to find seventh and eighth graders who had strong leadership potential. Such a test would be difficult under normal circumstances, but in this case the superintendent of the schools had already selected a test based entirely on reading. In most of his classes the African Americans and Hispanics were far behind in reading skills, so they tested low in leadership skills. Interestingly, the school board understood the problem. They authorized funds for another test, which enabled us to identify fairly and accurately those students with good leadership potential. This time African Americans and Hispanics were among those identified. It helps if examiners use a variety of instruments.

Determines If Students Understand Directions

A competent examiner will make an attempt to determine whether the child understands the directions. One reliable method is to ask the child questions to see if he or she understands. For example, suppose you are testing a child's ability to identify similarities between people or objects. To be sure that the child understands the concept, you could ask, "How are Michael Jordan and Walter Payton alike?" Acceptable answers would be "Both are black male athletes" or "Both played sports in Chicago." This will help clarify the child's understanding of what is being tested.

Inquires about the Child's Feelings

The examiner needs to notice if a child seems depressed. If possible, the examiner should talk to the child and include in the report that there are signs of depression. An examiner needs to know the signs of anxiety as well. The examiner will likely suggest more investigation and then additional testing.

Knows the Group's Heroes

In order to build rapport, trust, and respect with minority children, the examiner should be familiar with African American and Hispanic heroes—not just the people's names but also their accomplishments or contributions to society. When the children know that the examiner admires people like those the children admire, they will be more comfortable with the examiner.

Creates a Positive Atmosphere

The examiner should use all his or her skills to create a pleasant atmosphere that will help the children do their best work. If the examiner does not enjoy his or her job, the children will sense this negative attitude, and it will likely affect their performance. The examiner should want to be there and enjoy working with children of all ages and cultures.

Offers Praise

When appropriate, offer praise to the children. However, don't overdo it, as the children will sense the insincerity and will think you view them as "dumb." Give praise freely but only when it is justified.

Perhaps the most important piece of advice for examiners to remember is that disadvantaged children need all the help and encouragement they can get. These children start with a disadvantage because the tests were not made specifically for them; a testing approach that works for children who have had every advantage in life will often not work with them. Disadvantaged children need someone flexible and creative enough to find ways to answer their needs. While we psychologists stress a standardized approach, when we are dealing with those who are not a part of that standardized group, we need a new approach in order to be able to see their uniqueness.

THE CHILD—IMPROVING THE ODDS EVEN MORE

In life, as in test taking, we always want the odds in our favor. When we do that, we make ourselves "luckier." Often, when we take tests there are three to four answer choices. One choice is correct, one usually is nearly correct, and one or two are very wrong. By eliminating the obviously wrong answers, a child can increase his or her odds of success.

- We have said it before, but we are going to repeat it: guess the answer when you don't know. Don't leave the question incomplete.
- Pay attention to your first thought. It is often correct.
- Work on focusing and blocking what doesn't count.
- Look for the key. For example, how are a rabbit and dog alike? They both have fur, but the best answer is that they are animals. Look for the big or basic grouping.
- Analyze what is being asked.
- Look at the lives of famous people.
- Reword the question in your own words.
- Sometimes it helps to read the question and then look away and ask yourself, "What are they asking?"

Questions

Try your luck with the following by eliminating the bad answers. Then, judging from the remainder, choose the correct answer. Check the following pages for answers and analysis.

1. 2 is to 4, as 6 is to _____ ? (0, 1, 9, or 12)
2. 3 is to 4, as 9 is to _____ ? (10, 0, 81, or 9)
3. Brazil is what direction from Chicago? (west, east, north, or south)
4. Sun is to moon, as day is to _____? (night, January, cold, or hot)
5. 7 squared is _____? (0, 1, 49, or 14)
6. Water is to thirst, as food is to _____? (nutrient, nourish, hunger, or strength)
7. Man is to woman, as boy is to _____? (Daughter, Child, Girl, or Adult)
8. 7 is to 49, as 12 is to _____? (1, 19, 144, or 202)
9. Raspberry is to blueberry, as orange is to _____? (grape, raisin, peach, or lemon)
10. Car is to road, as boat is to _____? (travel, mechanical, water, or wind)

Answers and Analysis

Remember that we are trying to eliminate incorrect answers, to make selecting the right answer easier.

1. *The answers 0 and 1 are too small and are eliminated. The correct answer is 12 (2 doubled is 4: 6 doubled is 12).*
2. *The answers 0 and 81 are too large. Nine is no change, so 10 is the correct answer (3 plus 1 is 4: 9 plus 1 is 10).*
3. *We know that Brazil is warm, so the answer can't be north. The correct answer is south. We eliminate only one answer.*
4. *Sun and moon relate to the time of the day, not temperatures, so hot and cold are eliminated. The correct answer is night. We eliminate hot and cold, as they are temperatures. Night, like day, is a time of day.*
5. *Zero and 1 are too small, so we can eliminate them. The correct answer is 49.*
6. *We can eliminate the first two answers because they describe things that are done to the body, not what need is met. The correct answer is hunger. Food nourishes; therefore, hunger relates to food.*

7. *Eliminate the answers that deal with family relationships—man and woman are not family relations. The correct answer is girl, young like a boy.*

8. *Answers 1 and 19 are too small. The correct answer is 144. Based on 7 times 7, rule out the small numbers.*

9. *Raspberry and blueberry are types of berries. Grapes, raisins, and peaches are not citrus fruits like an orange. The correct answer is lemon. Note how you need to group things—for instance, not just fruit but citrus too.*

10. *The question is determining what the boat travels on. The first two answers do not allow things to travel on them. The correct answer is water.*

We hope from this little exercise you can see that two factors help bring success. The first is the children should carefully analyze the question, so they know what they need to answer. The second factor is to eliminate the very wrong answer and then guess the correct one.

SUMMARY

Examiners need to feel comfortable with minority children and have an understanding of their culture. Effective examiners are able to uncover the source of a child's test taking anxiety and to put a child at ease. Each child is unique, and examiners must be able to adapt their styles to match the child's needs; by the same token, when the child being tested is not a part of that standardized group, the examiner needs to alter his or her testing techniques. When the examiner creates a positive testing environment, children will relax, and their test scores are likely to rise. An examiner may be forced to use preselected tests, but he or she should be able to push for other, more culture-free tests that are more helpful. If tension is high, take a few breaks if possible.

Before children take a test, they should know what is expected of them and the purpose of the test. Some advice to children taking tests:

• Talk about any anxiety you may feel.
• Learn how to be a good guesser.
• Realize that no one test reveals everything about you.

- Try to have fun while taking the test.
- Use humor as a way to relax.
- Don't be afraid to ask questions.
- Slow down and think through the answers.
- Do the easy questions first and then do the hard ones.
- Think of your value as a person and know what you do well.
- Seek help when you need it.
- Seek specialized preparation (e.g., college entrance exams).
- Make up tests yourself to feel more comfortable.
- Analyze where weaknesses are (e.g., is it reading?).
- Work on concentration (see what we suggest).
- Refuse to give up. Remember that winners never quit!
- Try to improve your reading.
- Test yourself on what you've read.
- Practice timing yourself so you can be accurate in allowing a certain amount of time per test item.
- Share your feelings regarding achievement with friends, parents, and teachers.
- Tell your parents how they can support you for achievement.
- If your parents do not live together, go to each for areas in which they are particularly knowledgeable.
- Realize that a few failures are not going to ruin your life.
- Learn from test failures what you need to improve.

Improve your odds even more by doing the following.

- Guessing is a useful test-taking tool and strategy.
- Guessing improves your chances of receiving at least some credit.
- When you slow down and read the question carefully, at least two answers will reveal themselves as wrong.
- To overcome test anxiety, think of a past experience where you did well. Such an approach will help you relax and focus on a positive outcome.
- Think of tests as a game. Since games are fun, you'll likely do better if you regard the task as something you like.
- Practice your test-taking techniques by solving riddles. Riddles make you think, but they are fun, too.

9

TESTS CAN BE FUN

It has always seemed strange to me that in our endless discussions about education so little stress is laid on the pleasure of becoming an educated person, the enormous interest it adds to life. To be able to be caught up into the world of thought—that is to be educated.

—Edith Hamilton

People can have fun while taking tests and learning skills. Making testing fun can also lead to success. A joyful atmosphere stimulates learning and helps children so make them find a feeling of accomplishment.

Many people experience anxiety when they take a test. They become fearful and do not exert their best effort. In fact, some students show more anxiety taking a test than Michael Jordan did when facing a game-winning shot with one second left. To overcome his anxiety, Michael Jordan says, he simply concentrated on a past game in which he had done well. Such an approach helped him relax and focus on a positive outcome. You can use the same approach when it comes to testing. If you can see taking the test as fun and remember that you did well in the past, then experience is on your side. To show how fun testing can be, we suggest you practice taking tests by answering riddles. Here are some fun questions, beginning with riddles.

1. What is broken as soon as you say it?
2. The more you have, the worse you are. What is it?
3. What is the last word found in "lonesome"?
4. How are false teeth like stars?
5. Though not alive, it repeats what you say. What is it?
6. What is not alive but looks like your twin?
7. What has no life but grows?
8. What moves things but can't be seen?
9. What begins eternity and ends time?
10. It's metal but it flows. What is it?
11. What holds objects but can't be seen?
12. What has no beginning and no end?
13. What one thing can walk on all fours, twos, and threes?
14. What whispers to you but never says a word?

Answers to the riddles:

1. *Silence.*
2. *Debts.*
3. *Me.*
4. *They come out at night.*
5. *Echo.*
6. *Your reflection.*
7. *A crystal.*
8. *Wind.*
9. *The letter e.*
10. *Mercury.*
11. *Magnetism.*
12. *A circle.*
13 *Man—crawling, walking upright, then with a cane.*
14 *The wind.*

How about This? What Does It Mean?

At *ate* in the evening the Johnsons went *two* a store to buy *too* cartons of milk. Did they find what they wanted? Absolutely *knot*, and they *new* they wouldn't, because the stock was not *knew*. Answer: Keep changing the underlined words until you find what you feel is correct.

Problem Solving

This section aims at tasks that make people think. It is used to push people to look for a number of alternate answers and weigh which are better answers.

- What would you say to someone you knew had stolen from you?
- What makes lying so difficult?
- Can anger be useful at times? Explain.
- Can an argument be helpful?
- Why should you not leave your car running while you stop to buy a newspaper?
- Why should we let people have differences of opinion?

Abstractions: Classifying Things

How are these alike? What do they share? Answers help show how to reason abstractly.

Chair	Couch	Furniture	Sit in
Belt	Shoe	Clothes	Wear
Orange	Lemon	Citrus	Eat
Baseball	Theater	Entertainment	Watching
House	Home	Residence	Live in
Book	Paper	Education	Read
Letter	Number	Symbol	Colon
Slingshot	Tank	Weapon	Fight with
Wood	Metal	Material	Use it
Friendly	Irritable	Behavior	Social

Scoring: The third column is the abstract answer. It provides a classification system that allows putting things in groups.

Let's Learn from Proverbs

- A bird in the hand is worth two in a bush. (There is most value in what you can count on.)
- Look before you leap. (Think before you act.)
- The squeaky wheel gets the oil. (Persistent complainers—unfortunately—get attention.)
- A rolling stone gathers no moss. (Nothing slows the well prepared.)
- The apple never falls far from the tree. (We turn out much like our heritage.)
- You can't tell a book by its cover. (Superficial things give little reliable information.)
- Empty wagons make the most noise. (People who know little make worthless noise.)
- It takes two to tango. (It takes more than one to create a mess.)
- Don't be a pot that calls the kettle black. (Don't criticize others when you are as bad.)
- Big trees little acorns make. (Big things come from little things.)

TESTS THAT SHOW THE SUPERIORITY OF MINORITY CHILDREN

Strange that we defend our wrongs with more vigor than we do our rights.

—Kahlil Gibran

Most testing today is designed predominantly for the middle class and for the majority culture. See what happens when a test is designed differently. This is something we all should face from time to time. The tests in the chapter might help you gain more insight into how cultural deprivation, cultural differences, or lack of knowledge of the prevailing culture can affect test scores.

Robert L. Williams developed BITCH and SOB, he perhaps wanted to make a simple point. If African Americans perform poorly on tests with culturally loaded items, the same might be true when whites take a test that is culturally loaded with items pertaining to African American culture. For example, his test contains items of word knowledge (vocabulary) specific to African American culture and history. For example, the words such as "do rag" and "four corners" are more familiar to African American than their white counterparts. Similarly African American students would more likely answer questions such as "Who wrote the Negro national anthem?" correctly. A sample question is: What does "Running a game" mean?

a. Writing a bad check
b. Looking at something
c. Directing a contest
d. Getting what one wants from another person or thing.

Since both BITCH and SOB tests contain test items that are specific to African American words, expressions, and history, African Americans clearly performed better than whites on these tests. In contrast, SAT questions about a regatta are more likely to be answered correctly by white students who are more likely to be familiar with boating.

To prove that standardized tests can be culturally biased, we have devised a test that highlights common knowledge among minority children. Although not completely scientific, our findings to date show that black children excel at answering the questions below, while other children struggle. We urge you to take this test and see how you do. If you are African American, did you do well? If you are Caucasian, did you do poorly?

TEST FOR AFRICAN AMERICANS

Our goal is not to make a certain group of people feel bad about their knowledge. We simply wish to demonstrate how test bias can exist. Our ultimate hope is that soon there will be a set of standardized culture-free tests that give greater fairness to all test takers. Please do try the following test and encourage people of varying cultural backgrounds to try it as well.

Questions

1. Who was Booker T. Washington?
2. Who was Harriet Tubman?
3. What is Timbuktu?
4. What was the Underground Railroad?
5. What did Alex Haley do?
6. Who was Harriet Beecher Stowe?
7. Who was George Washington Carver?
8. Who is the number-one home run king?
9. How many products have been made from the peanut?

10. What are chitlins?
11. What is rap?
12. What direction from Algeria is Angola?
13. Where is Kenya?
14. What are greens?
15. When was African Americans first have the opportunity to work in an industry?
16. What are grits?
17. Who is Ice-T?
18. Who was Miles Davis?
19. Who was Chick Berry?
20. Name a African culture that was far advanced for its day.
21. Who is B. B. King?
22. Who was James Cotton?
23. What famous person declared, "I have a dream?"
24. Who was Frankie Lymon?
25. Name a high-ranking African American soldier.

Answers

1. *An educator who favored industrial education at a time when it was not available to all.*
2. *A woman who worked with the Underground Railroad.*
3. *A famous, highly advanced early civilization.*
4. *A covert escape route for by which southern black slaves reached the North.*
5. *He wrote the book* Roots.
6. *The author of* Uncle Tom's Cabin.
7. *He was a famous scientist. He found many uses for peanuts and sweet potatoes.*
8. *Henry Aaron.*
9. *Thanks to Dr. Carver, over three hundred.*
10. *A food product made from pig intestines.*
11. *A type of music.*
12. *South.*
13. *In Africa.*
14. *A food boiled and served as a vegetable.*

15. *During World War I.*
16. *A white corn product.*
17. *A modern musical performer.*
18. *A highly gifted trumpet player.*
19. *A famous guitar player.*
20. *Timbuktu.*
21. *A famous blues singer and guitar player.*
22. *A gifted harmonica player.*
23. *Dr. Martin Luther King, Jr.*
24. *A famous contemporary singer.*
25. *Gen. Colin Powell, before his retirement.*

TEST FOR HISPANICS

Questions

1. What is *albondigas*?
2. What is Cinco De Mayo?
3. Who is Carlos Santana?
4. Who was Ellen Ochoa?
5. What is Octlan? Jalisco?
6. Who is Jimmy Smits?
7. To what does Rio Grand refer?
8. What is Menudo?
9. What is unusual about the Hispanic writing of dates?
10. When is Mexican Independence Day?
11. What was Nancy Lopez famous for?
12. Who is Ricky Martin?
13. Who was Poncho Villa?
14. What is the significance of the of the Alamo?
15. Who is Rita Moreno?
16. Who is Vicente Fox?
17. Who was Lorenzo Meyer?
18. Who was Carlos Fuentes?
19. What is *"el Ojo"*?
20. Who was Roberto W. Clemente?

21. Who is Julio Inglesias?
22. Who was Cesar Chavez?
23. Who is Julia Chavez?
24. Who was Luis Alvarez.?
25. Who was "Crying Lady—La Llorona"?
26. Who is Felix Trinidad?
27. Who is Lee Trevino?

Answers

1. *Meatball soup.*
2. *Independence Day.*
3. *Famous musician and first Hispanic inducted into the Rock and Roll Hall of Fame.*
4. *First female Hispanic astronaut, 1990.*
5. *A city and state of Mexico.*
6. *Famous TV actor.*
7. *Large river that divides Mexico and Texas.*
8. *Soup made with tripe.*
9. *It uses no capitalization (all lower case).*
10. *May 5th.*
11. *First female Hispanic golfer to be inducted into the Hall of Fame.*
12. *A well known singer.*
13. *A conqueror.*
14. *Early battle in the Mexican-American War.*
15. *Actress and dancer, only performer to win an Oscar, Tony, Emmy, and Grammy (1979).*
16. *President of Mexico.*
17. *Well known historian.*
18. *A famous Hispanic author.*
19. *A superstition that pretty children must be touched or they will become ill.*
20. *Born in Puerto Rico, he became the first Hispanic voted into the Baseball Hall of Fame.*
21. *Well known worldwide singer, received the first Diamond Record Award.*

22. *Leader, reformer of the United Farm Workers, awarded the Presidential Medal of Freedom (highest civilian award).*
23. *Famous prizefighter.*
24. *In 1968 developed a narrow-band radar that allow planes to operate more safely in bad weather; won the Nobel Prize.*
25. *A myth that a murdered girl cries at night.*
26. *Famous boxer.*
27. *Famous Hispanic golfer.*

SUMMARY

- Each culture excels at answering certain types of questions.
- Share your culture knowledge with others so everyone can gain a greater understanding and respect for those who are different from them.

11

PSYCHING UP AND BATTLING THE VARIOUS TESTS: SPECIFIC REMEDIES

In preceding chapters we addressed and evaluated procedures involved in test construction; types of psychological, education, and aptitude tests; and inherent test biases embedded in many psychoeducation tests. We also outlined the role of various important individuals (e.g., parents, teachers, and educators) and organizations (e.g., schools and education system) that indirectly affect the performance of minority students on various tests. We talked about the significant role of socioeconomic factors to indirectly affect the poor performance of minority students. We discussed various social and economic factors, including sociocultural background, social and geographical segregation, family systems, school systems, poverty, single-parent households, and teenage parents, which produce an indirect but significant impact on test performance. We proposed and recommended that society as a whole can provide remedies to these issues that are likely to affect the test performance of minority students. This chapter deals with variables specific to test taking and may provide direct help for minority students. We will provide direct suggestions that are likely to help minority students improve their test scores.

HOW TO PSYCHE UP MINORITY STUDENTS

Minority students often have to develop an inner strength, so a good technique for them is called "psyching." Athletes use it; why not students? Here is a rough idea how it works. The student focuses as much as possible on some target to get in the desired mood. For example, if he wants to be calmer he might envision walking along a deserted beach with waves breaking over the shore. But he'll need to work to actually see the scene in his mind. If he can't get sufficiently into an "upbeat" frame of mind, he might focus on seeing himself running with the football during a game. As you develop this technique, you'll get where you see yourself in the action. This approach is very adaptable for test taking because people tend to go to extremes when taking tests. If you're too fast, you'll be careless; if you're too slow, you don't get done. For each person, there is an ideal place.

A similar use of psyching involves low esteem and test taking. The following is a case in point. Bob admitted that he felt dumb in school and later unqualified for any good job. He reported that every job he applied for has some sort of test. He couldn't take the pressure and stopped applying, later accepting a low-paying, physical job that he hated. He eventually, through a friend, got into a psyching program. He pictured himself as competent and bright, and found that he felt more confident. His approach to people and tests become much more competent, and he now has a job that he loves.

The Case of Psyching Jordan

The application of psyching can best be illustrated by the following counseling treatment program. A 13-year-old boy, Jordan, came with his mother to our clinic seeking help, yet feeling he was beyond help. His school grades were inconsistent, ranging from high average to failing. Of late, his teachers began to feel that he didn't care. One of his teachers went so far as to say that "some of these kids just take up space."

Jordan was also suspended from school for fighting, even though it was established that the other teenager made a very nasty racial slur. To make matters worse, the other boy received a shorter suspension because he had a higher grade-point average. One of his teachers defended him: "Jaime came from a better family, he's done well in his classes, and he's going to college. Jordan won't come close."

Other things continued to go badly for Jordan. He applied for a job and lost out to two other boys from a different cultural background. He did recognize that he had low self-esteem. Jordan felt that it related to his hard-working father who seldom had time for the family. It seemed to Jordan that he was a hard worker in a low-paying position with little chance to get ahead.

This looked like a hopeless situation, but sometimes it takes only one person to make a change. Jordan attended a program offered through our clinic that had to do with availability. What is *availability*? In order to receive help, a person must be accessible. Many people are afraid of change and won't listen. Jordan listened and heard about people who won't be helped when they need it. That didn't make sense to Jordan. "Why would someone refuse help?" Jordan asked himself over and over again. Then all of a sudden Jordan remembered his own behavior with a teacher, Mrs. Jones, who tried to help him. He concluded that he was afraid of help. "Why?" he wondered. More often than not, it is a rejection of the social system or a result of low self-esteem. When you have low self-esteem, you live with the fear that others will find out you're not smart.

By the time Jordan had two sessions, he began to see some improvement. He learned that self-esteem is the way you see yourself, and it tells you what you feel you can accomplish. As a general rule, people who think poorly of themselves give up easily. After a few more sessions, Jordan suffered some setbacks. With these defeats he realized that he had low self-esteem. Although he was in the uncomfortable position of recognizing that he had what he thought of as a significant personality flaw, because of his counseling he knew that something had changed— namely that now he wanted to find out why he had low self-esteem and correct it. He remembered the teacher who had been so kind to him and so interested in him, Mrs. Jones. But by the time Jordan contacted Mrs. Jones, he was both depressed and angry. It started when he went to apply for a job that sounded good to him and he was required to fill out an application and take a short test. Jordan was positive that he had done well on the test, yet he was rejected. He concluded that he was rejected because he had the "wrong skin color." He did admit later, however, that anxiety had hampered him when he took the test. Jordan began to feel very discouraged, like nothing he could do could ever make him right for a really good job.

So when Jordan arrived at Mrs. Jones's office he was not in a very upbeat mood. Mrs. Jones sensed that and allowed Jordan to talk out some of his feelings of anger and what it was that had particularly discouraged him. She was impressed by how he organized his description of what had taken place.

When he finished speaking, he sat back waiting for Mrs. Jones to respond. He waited for a few moments and then asked her, "Well, what now?"

Mrs. Jones looked directly at Jordan, making eye contact, and said to him, "I know you're right and these things happen in our society, but the big question is 'What are you going to do about it?' " Jordan quickly responded, with some irritation, "What can I do about it?"

Mrs. Jones answered Jordan's challenge. "Actually, Jordan, there is a lot you can do about it and I'm going to make a suggestion for a beginning. Instead of seeing yourself as a loser and a victim, I want you to think of yourself as a worrier. You're going to have a fight ahead because it's hard to change the world, but little by the little, if you take a position of strength and motivation, you can do it."

Jordan began to feel a ray of hope and asked Mrs. Jones where he could get started. Mrs. Jones responded this time by saying, "The starting point is to help you feel strong, and that requires powerful self-esteem." With the help of Mrs. Jones and those who cared, Jordan began building the following *foundations for success*:

Positive self-esteem. Mrs. Jones responded carefully and meticulously by indicating that if you have low self-esteem, you give up quickly and only half try. You project weakness. She had directions for Jordan that he needed to follow: "Jordan, I want you to start with the resolve that you won't make any negative, self-critical remarks. Every time you say that you can't do something or that you're not bright, I want you to put a quarter aside, which will go in the jar right here on my desk. Second, I want you to write down your accomplishments—things you're proud of, things that you've done in your short lifetime. I want you to pin those up by the mirror where you get up and dressed in the morning, as a reminder of the good things that you've done."

Warrior determination. Mrs. Jones went right back to work on Jordan's self-concept and motivation. "First of all, Jordan," she began, "I want you to realize that you're a member of a cultural group that has gone through a lot in the way of prejudice. That means that this group has to be strong to have survived this long. I think you certainly have that strength buried within you, and you can bring it forth on any particular occasion to direct yourself properly. I want you to psyche yourself up so you feel like a warrior, so you see yourself being powerful and very directed."

Motivation. Mrs. Jones explained to Jordan that with more opportunity, people can now dream about what they would like to do and be when they mature. No longer is there the degree of exclusion of particular groups because of their cultural background and heritage. Therefore, there is more reason then ever before that if you're motivated and can drive yourself toward achievement, there is a much greater likelihood that you'll reach your goals."

Coping with prejudice. Mrs. Jones responded to Jordan's worries about prejudice right away. "Yes, Jordan, there are some times where pure prejudice keeps you shut out of something, but there are fewer of those all of the time. Now is the time to learn test-taking techniques so you're strong and have a good opportunity to present yourself in a favorable light. Yes, it is true that tests can be slanted toward some cultures and not others, but at least you have more of a fighting chance now than minorities did in the past. Make yourself strong with test-taking skills and don't focus excessively on the negative aspects. Remember, Jordan, that you can't change the world overnight and you can't do anything about making tests culturally unbiased, but you can make yourself as strong as you can possibly be by using the correct methods to build strength."

In the weeks that followed, Jordan showed increasing skill in pursuing the approaches that Mrs. Jones had recommended. He began to look for more places to build his strength and to gain information so he could direct himself more adequately towards certain kinds of goals. Some of the *specific techniques* that he used were as follows:

Communication. Jordan realized one day that by talking to students who had just taken a particular test, he would have a better idea of what he needed to know and how to improve his test-taking skills. He developed the approach that he was going to learn from the mistakes of other people.

The Internet. Jordan learned that the Internet is free and that he could get wonderful information from it. He could get short tests that would allow him to become used to test taking so his anxiety level would drop.

Parents. Jordan learned that he could get help from his parents in a way that he had never thought of before. It was true that they worked such long hours that they couldn't do a lot of things for him or with him, but they could encourage him. He found his father to be very skilled in establishing a stress-free environment, particularly when Jordan was trying to learn something and prepare for a job opportunity or test.

Practice testing. Jordan learned that some of the important tests, such as college entrance tests, often provide a sample test that you can take home and practice with. By looking at these sample tests, you had a better idea of what you would need to learn in order to pass.

Job experience. Jordan learned that it helped to talk to people in different jobs to get a better impression of what those jobs are like. He lost interest in some and became more interested in others because of what he found out.

Library. Jordan soon learned that libraries were free and that he could get important information there. Additionally, some bookstores allow customers to come in and browse without having to buy anything.

Differential reinforcement. Jordan found that he felt better when he earned a particular reward for doing something he was supposed to. It seemed to work very well for him that he could do something special on those occasions where he had made an appropriate, positive advancement. This could be anything from a movie to a pizza—not necessarily a major reinforcer, but just enough to provide a reward to increase incentive and thereby motivation. When he found himself slacking, he would give up something that he wanted to do that day.

Transfer of learning. Jordan was encouraged to apply something he learned in one area to other activities. This transfer of learning meant that he was using the new information he had obtained, in a variety of ways. This also tended to make him more flexible as far as problem-solving activities were concerned.

Sharpening skills. Jordan learned that he could improve his social skills by interacting more with people. It just became easier and easier as his self-esteem work progressed. Talking to other people helped him expand his vocabulary, and understanding why other people act the way they do improved his comprehension and reasoning capabilities. Jordan practiced by the hour, sitting in a room, screening out extraneous sounds. He also had his mother read numbers to him at an even pace as he practiced, so he could concentrate better and heighten his working memory.

Other books. From reading other books, Jordan found more and more ways to solve problems and be flexible in his learning approaches.

Jordan found that he was becoming a more positive person because he had more approaches to solving problems. He went back to visit Mrs. Jones after not seeing her for a few of months, and told her about his decision to go to a junior college. As things got even better for him, he decided to try to get a scholarship for college. Ultimately, Jordan showed himself to be a true warrior who sets a goal and then pursues it through all adversity.

The Case of Psyching José

A case of a Hispanic seventeen-year-old student named as José who dropped out of school for a number of reasons can also illustrate psyching a student for success. José was born to Mexican immigrant parents who came to America with a lot of difficulties, in search of a better life for themselves and their children. Like many immigrant families do, his parents found a place to live in a predominantly Hispanic, east Chicago neighborhood. His parents found themselves at home, as they were able to go to the grocery store, open a bank account, go to the post office, and carry out their daily activities without having to speak any English. Even his father's first job as a laborer didn't require that he speak English.

José meanwhile started going to a bilingual school. He gradually picked up some words in English and began to attend English as a second language (ESL) classes. Soon he was able to communicate with his American friends. As expected, José attained basic proficiency in English rather quickly, but at home he communicated in Spanish with his parents, who barely spoke English. He witnessed his parents going through the financial stress and cultural trauma of living in a new country. His father was unable to pass his driver's test until he took a test in Spanish. His four brothers and sisters spent a lot of time without supervision, as both parents worked and did not have the adequate means to hire a babysitter. Many times these children were left unsupervised.

José struggled with his homework and didn't receive any help from his parents, because of their lack of time and formal education. José's role model, his father, was a hard-working man who knew only how to be a laborer. His uncles and aunts had similar lives. During family get-togethers, José experienced all aspects of the Hispanic culture, including food, language, and values. For many years José did not come into contact with the world outside his culture. In his neighborhood he could get by communicating in Spanish, hanging out with peers from his own culture, watching Spanish speaking TV channels, and learning the Hispanic social structure.

Due to financial constraints in the family, José had to drop out of school to help out the family financially. He completed the ninth grade but was unable to complete the tenth grade. José, however, was motivated to "be somebody." He was intelligent and curious and wanted to have experiences beyond his culture and language. He wanted to live the "American dream," but his first priority was to go out and get a job. Initially he had to work illegally, as he couldn't attain a work permit due to his age. In the back of his mind, however, he knew that he wasn't going to end up working as a laborer like his father for the rest of his life.

He decided to complete his GED but he didn't know where to start. He contacted his old teacher, who was very kind to him and agreed to advise him how to proceed. He didn't know that he could use many free academic sources, for example books geared towards GED preparation from a public library. Once his mentor advised him to tap these resources, he was able to learn from these books and also the Internet, to prepare for the exam.

Unfortunately, he soon found himself being made fun of. His parents didn't think he was capable of graduating from high school, his peers began to call him a "nerd" who wants to act like a "white boy." Negativity about the pursuit of his goal was everywhere around him. But his motivation was to get out of poverty. He realized that his peers and family didn't care if he graduated from high school because they assumed he was going to be a laborer. He also realized that there were only two ways to get out of poverty—and one of the ways was education. The second was hitting a lottery jackpot or becoming a professional football player, neither of which he through was very realistic.

Once he made up his mind and obtained the right resources, he set aside the time to study and began to seek help from those who had graduated from high school. He began to associate himself with positive people who encouraged him to follow his goals.

It is evident that José cannot go back and change his environment, poverty, lack of healthcare, poor schooling, incompetent teachers, lack of enriched environment, lack of adequate role models, lack of parental involvement in his academic life, crowded classrooms, bilingual disadvantage, peer pressure, inadequate academic resources such as computers and the Internet, exposure to violence and drugs, and above all direct or indirect prejudice of some members of the majority group. However, he *can* do a number of things to achieve his goals, as described in the following sections of this chapter.

HOW TO TAKE TESTS: LEARNING THE NATURE OF THE TEST

The starting point for preparing for test taking means asking questions such as "What is the purpose of the particular test?" "How is the test being used?" "Is any study recommended or available for this particular test-taking experience?" and "What are the consequences for the particular test?" For example the results of taking a college entrance exam are clear-cut and can seriously affect your future. Not knowing how a particular test is going to be used and what the consequences of your score are is a source of anxiety. It's always worse to know that something important is taking place but not to know exactly what than it is to know specifically what you have to be concerned about. Fear of the unknown is generally much more destructive than most things we do know about. Consequently, information should be provided to people taking a test as to *how the test results are going to be used and what their consequences are*. Also, you want to know if there are alternate tests you can take if you have difficulty with the one being presented on that specific occasion. As a matter of fact, taking a similar test before you take the one that counts can be very helpful. It shows you what to expect and how you'll need to perform.

Another important bit of information that should be provided is whether *wrong* answers count against your performance. Usually they don't, but with some college entrance exams they do (e.g., the SAT). Apparently, this is done to discourage guessing, but those who feel some insecurity about the guessing process are going to suffer more than those who are familiar with it. The point is to be sure that you know whether there are limitations as far as wrong answers are concerned.

Also, it is extremely important to know whether the task has a *time limit* to it. If it does, you need to know what the limit is and can therefore prepare for it. For example, with multiple-choice tests, you want to know how many minutes or seconds you have for each answer. This will determine, to a great extent, what your planning approach is when going through the task at hand.

PRACTICAL STRATEGIES TO ENHANCE TEST SCORES

Regardless of whether the test you're going to take will determine which school or college you go to or whether you qualify for a scholarship or can graduate from high school, a certain amount of preparation is required:

Develop a study plan. a study plan in advance of tests such as the SAT is vital to your success in the exam. Try completing the entire course work at least two weeks ahead of time, so you have sufficient time for a review. Don't try to learn new information the day before the exam.

Have a proctor. If you're taking a time-sensitive test, it's a good idea to have a proctor who can monitor you when you practice.

Get ready using duplicate testing conditions. Study at the same time of the day you'll take the real test. It helps with mental preparation. Also, have as few distractions as possible.

Test yourself. Since you're preparing for a big test, it's a good idea to set some dates when you want someone to give you a mock test. After each chapter, a brief mock test in a similar testing situation will help you to gain confidence. This will also help you sharpening your test-taking skills. A number of websites allow you to take these practice tests for no cost.

Reward yourself. Do some of your favorite things, such as watching TV or playing basketball, once you accomplish a chapter or section. Don't try to accomplish too much in too little time. Take one step at a time. Stepwise learning has been found to be a better technique.

Don't overwhelm yourself. Pace your studying, and take the necessary number of breaks.

Have a study buddy. The study buddy system is extremely helpful. If a friend or acquaintance is taking the same or similar test, you can prepare together.

Teach your mind to be flexible. We are generally taught to engage in problem-solving in a certain way. Always look for an alternative or different approach to solving a problem.

Rest and nourishment are as important as studying. Above all, it's highly recommended that you get a good night's rest the night before and a good breakfast the morning of a test. After all, the body also has to be prepared to respond to pressure, and it can do that best if it's well prepared with sleep and an adequate amount of food.

Develop a positive attitude and outlook. Reading about those who overcame adversity helps. Identify an adult who has overcome adversity and whom you admire. Learn about that person's positive strategies for overcoming disadvantages.

Identify what's good about you. Ask family and friends what they like about you. Write down all your good qualities and put the paper where you'll see it. In the case of José, he might want to recall that he did not drop out of school because he was academically incompetent, but because of the financial circumstances of the family. His motivation to succeed and strong desire to accomplish his goals and get out of an environment in which he doesn't feel comfortable are his positive assets.

Examine your accomplishments. Ask yourself what you've achieved, e.g., bringing up your grades, joining an academic or sports group, reading more, or feeling more motivated. Anything that adds a positive value to yourself, society, or your family is an accomplishment. So get some successes under your belt! Start working on easy things first to boost courage and strengthen determination.

Tap your inner sources. Each one of us has an inner strength that we ignore or don't even know exists. Turn inwards for strength and determination with the help of those you can trust.

Pay attention to success stories around you. In magazines, newspapers, and your neighborhood success stories abound. Look around and listen more carefully to those who have succeeded and ask them for help or advice. Older adults such as teachers and elders in the community will be only too eager to share their stories.

Cultivate curiosity. Small children tend to be hugely curious about the world and things around them. Yet as they grow they lose this wonderful quality, are reprimanded when they're distracted by their surroundings, and are told to focus. This quality of curiosity that leads to so much learning in early childhood, however, is important for success in later life. It has not disappeared; it is merely suppressed. So encourage your inner curiosity to emerge with books and knowledge.

Remind yourself that knowledge is power. Research has shown that it isn't only the number of cells in your brain that is important, but the rich network of communication between the brain cells. The more knowledge, the richer the network. So read, ask questions, and learn as much as you can about your school subjects and research on the Internet and journals. This will help you not only with memory and increasing your IQ, but also to *develop other strategies* more easily.

Attention and concentration are two vital components of learning. Attention improves with a neutral environment. It isn't important how many hours you study; the important thing is that you're giving one hundred percent when you *are* studying. Find the environment that make you concentrate better. Whether a park or your room, designate one place that reminds you of only one thing—to study and prepare for your exam. It's important, however, to make a change if you become bored studying at the same place.

Develop cognitive strategies. Teach yourself ways to retain information, or individualized strategies. Anyone can develop and use these kind of strategies. For example, while trying to remember a paragraph, use visual imagery to remember name, place, or event. Or associate the paragraph with a life event. Or convert the information into auditory data, e.g., hear yourself explain the concept to someone else.

***Retain* and *recall* are first cousins.** If you remember placing your book on the desk in your room, you'll recall it when you need it. If you didn't pay attention when putting the book down, it's unlikely that you'll be able to recall its location. Another example is that if you're sitting in a car and looking outside the window but thinking of something else, it's unlikely you'll be able to recall whether you passed by a McDonald's. But if you were paying attention, you'll be able to recall when and where you saw the restaurant. This can be referred to as *not forgetting to remember*.

Learn retrieval and retention strategies. A calm and quiet brain can recall better than a noisy and anxious brain. This is why it's very important that your mind is calm in the examination hall. Anxiety is the number-one enemy of recall. Stress, distraction, life events, extreme anxiousness to succeed, unusual competitiveness, and unrealistic expectations are all intruders to your optimum performance.

Use auditory and visual repetition. Repetition and practice are vital for learning. The brain can learn new things subconsciously. It's a good method to provide your brain with auditory input while you're doing something else, like listening to music. Even if you don't remember everything, you'll soon find that the answers come to you more easily. Similarly, you might want to provide yourself with a visual aid by writing post-it notes to yourself. Put these notes in places where you can easily see them. Constant visual input facilitates new learning.

Reflect on what you've learned. It's always a good idea to take a walk or relax after learning a new chapter, and (without cues) recall as much as you can from this newly learned chapter.

Use your sense organs effectively. The brain has five sensory modalities, and you might want to use all these modalities effectively to get the maximum out of your brain. Children often use only one modality, such as visual, but fail to use the other senses. For example, use audio books or repeat information out loud. As mentioned previously, repetitive learning is an excellent tool. If books on tape are available, you might want to borrow some from a library.

Break information down into parts/steps. This strategy helps you learn more easily, as smaller pieces of information can be more easily absorbed by the brain.

Treat your brain like an instrument. You want to get the maximum out of your brain. The more you know about the way your brain functions, the more you can get out of it. It's worthwhile knowing how the brain perceives, receives, and retains information. The brain is like a computer, without a manual. In the last few decades we've learned much about the human brain. The more José and Jordan know about the functional organization of the brain and ways to get the maximum out of it, the more advantages they'll have. The more we give the brain, the more we can get out of it—like loading software in a computer. Also, the brain is quick to learn information when it's presented like a story with a be-

ginning, middle, and end. *Incoherent* and *rote learning* require extra effort because it has no pattern. Information that's musical and rhythmic,
or information with a visual pattern and colors, will easily stick to the
brain. Our brain does not like interference in its new learning (also called
retroactive inhibition). If you just learned a new theorem, you don't want
to learn another theorem immediately. This would interfere in your new
learning. In fact, it's a good idea to either pause for a while or do something fun, completely unrelated to what you've just learned.

If you can't beat them, join them in their success. Every school has
students who do well. Join these successful students in their study group, or,
if you find it easier, create a study group with other students like yourself.

Overcome prejudice obstacles. José has always felt that he's at a disadvantage compared to white children. There are racial prejudices at least
at the subconscious level that cannot be completely overcome. José cannot
change that, but what he can do is to strive to excel and be at least at par
with majority students by combining his intellect and hard work. Professionals such as physicians and university professors commonly command
the same respect from their students and colleagues as their majority counterparts, provided they're competent and work hard at what they do.

Recognize when the brain needs rest. Our human brain is like
any man-made machine. Like an engine requires oil changes and tune
ups, the human brain also needs regular maintenance. For example, the
brain requires rest. José and Jordan should be sensitive to the fact that
their brains are tired and can't take in more information. One sign of
tiredness is when you find yourself staring at a sentence or word and
know that you're no longer able to read it clearly. You might even become dizzy. A good night's sleep, mentally less strenuous activity for a
while, humor, laughter, and nourishment are important needs of this human instrument. Make sure you take care of your brain's needs.

TEST PREPARATION MAY BE A SKILL, BUT TEST TAKING IS AN ART

Many students prepare well but they don't do as well as expected
in a test because of their poor test-taking skills. Test anxiety, fatigue, im-

pulsive decisions, or rushing to finish the test are some of the factors that can lower your test score even though you may be very well prepared.

Face, not escape. During the beginning stages of the test preparation, you might feel overwhelmed, but gradually you'll begin to gain control on your test-taking skills and preparation.

Learn to stick to your study schedule. Make sure that you don't derail from your study habits. Just as our bodies demand nourishment, you must train your mind to be hungry to finishing a book or chapter.

Let your family/friends join in your endeavor. Once you decide that you're going to stick to your schedule, let your family and friends know that during your study hours, no demands in terms of your time can be made. By fostering this understanding, you're inviting them to help you with your endeavor, and you won't feel lonely.

Knowledge is power. Knowledge is a powerful tool that not only helps you achieve what you want but also command respect from others, regardless of their age, sex, or racial background.

Coping with anxiety. Preparing for a test is not punishment. Remember that *high test anxiety lowers performance.* We strongly recommend people preparing to take tests develop some sort of workable *relaxation program.* We suggest Jacobson's progressive muscle relaxation, which progressively relaxes your body by having you tighten and loosen muscle groupings. A short relaxation program could be simply inhaling fully and then gradually exhaling. Taking a deep breath is one easy technique for quick relaxation that has worked for many people. Taking tests makes everyone nervous, so it's important to know how to handle it. You don't want to be afraid to admit that you feel tension because then you can't do anything to alleviate the tension.

In brief—set easy achievable goals, find out what motivates you, realize that there's time for play and time for studying, create a positive environment, have discussions with family members/friends, teach others, display new learning, be inquisitive, ask yourself what you've learned, use mental strategies to lower stress and improve learning, learn to increase your speed of learning, set start and finish time, practice good study habits, identify a successful role model, use the group model of studying, and ask your parents to encourage you to study.

STRATEGIES FOR THE DAY OF THE TEST

On the Day of the Test

If there's a time gap between the two parts of a two-part test, make sure you eat a light healthy meal during the break, avoid discussing the previous portion of the exam with friends, and relax in a quiet environment.

Taking the Test

When prepared to take the test, first find answers to the following questions: "What is the purpose of this particular test?" and "What does it mean to me?" Then determine the nature of the exam—is it a multiple-choice, recall, or essay test? After that question has been answered, the next thing you want to know is how many items there are and how long you'll have to respond. While taking the test, try to finish items that are easier first; once you answer those, you'll have more confidence for the harder questions. Try not to spend too much time on any one problem. Keep track of how much time you've spent and how much time you have left. Family members should be encouraging and comforting, providing positive reinforcements during the preparation period. The tone should be positive, such as "I'm sure your preparation is going well," "I'm confident you'll do well," "You seem to be well prepared," or "I wouldn't worry too much about the test—just do your best."

HOW TO TAKE THE VARIOUS TESTS

Recall Test

The *recall test* is the most difficult to respond to and be successful with, as it relies largely on retrieval of information from memory. This type of test might involve initiating retrieval and storage strategies. What it really hinges on is your memory, particularly "medium-term"—not short-term memory and it certainly not long-term memory. People who have difficulty with memory items are likely to find the recall system to be most difficult. After you know how much time is allotted for each item, go through the test in rapid order in almost a semiconscious manner. In other words, read the items quickly and respond as well as you can at that particular point, attempting to remain calm even when some of the tasks are difficult. It may help to realize that everyone finds recall test difficult because you're pulling things out of memory. Keep in mind that very often you can intuitively or unconsciously come up with a correct answer if given a chance to do so. It's when you try to force the brain to find information that difficulties arise. Consequently, approaching this sort of a test as if it were a more relaxed, casual type of activity is most helpful much of the time.

After you've gone through test the first time in a relatively quick manner, go back over each of the items that are important to you, for whatever reason, and attempt to recheck your work. These would be items that you're not certain you have the right answer to and you want to recheck your thinking, but be very careful! It's easy to check something that was answered correctly and change it to an incorrect answer because you thought about it too hard. Try to learn to trust your memory and your general ability to respond to the various tests.

Finally, attempt to find out which answers you got correct and which ones you didn't get correct. This is very important because if you didn't do as well you wanted, you might need to take the test again. Knowing where you failed or fell short will allow you to prepare next time in a different sort of manner. It might also show you where you tend to go off in your answers. For example, do you tend to be too technical or too rigidly specific? If you do, you might want to try a different approach next time so you're not responding so rigidly to the task.

Essay Test

A second major form of test taking is the essay test. This kind of test gives individuals instructions to provide information, almost like a story, in answer to various questions. Our first bit of advice would be that you try to *clearly understand* what the individual who designed the test is asking. What does he want you to say that would give you a correct response? One of the mistakes that many test takers make is to cover everything under the sun, including things that are mutually incompatible.

For example, on one occasion we used the test question "What are the implications of physical activity on bodily functioning?" A particular test taker could very easily have talked about such things as blood pressure, heart rate, level of tension, and so forth, but instead chose focus on the economics of sporting activity—concluding that being athletic can affect a person's work accomplishments. His argument was that if you play a good game of golf, it will help you in the business world. So it may, but it doesn't have a relationship to bodily functioning as a result of physical exercise. It was a worthy topic, bit too cluttered. Ultimately, the person taking the test lost out, to some extent, because of his overly diverse approach towards answering. You must keep in mind that with the essay test, you have to find out what the individual is asking for and then come up with a game plan to provide it. It's highly recommended that the test taker write an *outline* on scrap paper when confronted by this type of test so he can be organized and goal-directed.

Another point to recognize is that teachers and professors consider certain pieces of information to be particularly important. If you can identify what these particular points are, you have a much greater chance of mentioning them in your essay evaluation than if you're going in somewhat blindly. A case in point would be if one of a teacher's major points in a psychology class was that psychology is a science. If you were to state, in an essay test, that the definition of psychology is "a discipline that studies behavior, a discipline that could be philosophy or, for that matter, theology" then you would have missed out on this teacher's point. Finally, when dealing with an essay test, try to keep answers related specifically to the stated question rather than putting in everything in and making it too long. Anyone grading the test will soon grow tired of the task if it goes on and on without clearly and concisely getting to the point.

Multiple-Choice Test

By far the most popular of the test formats in use today is the *multiple-choice test*. Again, all of the things mentioned earlier in this chapter still apply: relaxation is important, so is attention, and so is an ability to concentrate. You need to know time limits, what is expected, and what the purpose of the test will be. It is recommended that the test taker go through the test questions in a relatively rapid fashion and to put question marks next to those with uncertain answers. It is important to know whether wrong answers count against you. It is also important to know whether time is a factor, in other words whether you get time bonuses or whether there is simply one lump sum of time you can use or not use at your discretion while taking the test.

As you go through the test items, be sure to immediately cross out definitely wrong choices for questions where you're not sure about your answer. You're probably going to have to make a guess for these, and your odds are a lot better when you're guessing one out of three or two than one out of four or five. Again, keep in mind the idea that you'll often be correct intuitively, and your first choice is not necessarily a bad one. Be very careful second- and even third-guessing answers, where you may overly analyze and thereby make an error.

If wrong answers don't count against you, then you need to make some guesses. Otherwise, you're simply throwing away the possibility of raising your score. It's important to realize that with some test situations, you're not being asked which answer is correct but rather which answer is more correct than the other answers. If that's the case, guessing again becomes very important. Always keep in mind that you want to raise your odds. Tests make everyone nervous; the important thing is how you handle that nervousness.

In summary, keep in mind that no test is an absolute be-all or end-all. If you have difficulty taking tests, then you might need to work gradually on approaches that will allow you to relax more. You might also want to find resources so you can study in preparation for particular tests. Always have faith in yourself, and keep in mind that no test is a perfect way to select out those who are skilled from those who are not. Every test has a relatively high degree of inaccuracy.

True-False Tests

Another type of test commonly used is the true-false test. This test draws somewhat on memory, but it relies more on recognition. Relaxation is important, so use what we have recommended in preceding sections. Then do *not* look for perfect answers—look for what is more true than false. Don't be a perfectionist! Watch the false answers; they're easier to spot because the answers are less logical. Here are some strategies for handling this type of test:

- Try to keep in mind the perspective of the person who made the tests, if possible.
- Guess when necessary.
- Answer easy items first.
- Listen to your unconscious mind.
- Practice test taking so you're familiar with the process.
- Reward your performance with something you like.
- Keep in mind that with true-false questions, you have only one wrong answer to eliminate.
- Reorient your approach if necessary. For example, one student approached us with the following problem with a true-false test: "Both answers seem very wrong—I could find something wrong with all answers," he declared. We suggested that he look for the "least wrong answer," and with that approach he did well.
- Talk out your answers—this can often give you another viewpoint.
- True-false questions are usually short, which can temp you to answer too quickly.
- Keep a comfortable pace.
- Check your time limits—work accordingly.
- Note your first impressions.
- Envision yourself as being up to handling this challenge.
- If you're confused, ask "Where have I heard this before?"
- With the majority of questions, ask "What is the question trying to ask?"
- Try to come away from the test with an idea of what you need to study further.

Problem-Solving Tests

Some tests involve an actual problem-solving challenge. Here are some helpful approaches.
- Try to understand the problem.
- Break problems into segments.
- Use a flexible approach.
- Evaluate your performance. Is your approach working?
- Do you need to change your approach?
- Outline what you need to do to solve the problem.

- Where are you headed?
- What have you learned that bears on the test.
- Evaluate what constitutes a "solved" problem.
- What is the goal you're trying to reach?
- Can you come up with a creative approach?
- When you finish the test, have you answered all the questions involved?

In sum, there are different types of tests, and different strategies are needed to handle each kind of test. Proper test preparation and review, mock test taking, and knowledge of the type and content of the test to be taken can all lead to successful testing.

EPILOGUE

Kalyani Gopal

If you are planning for a year, sow rice; if you are planning for a decade, plant trees; if you are planning for a lifetime, educate people.

—Chinese proverb

Throughout our American society, we have segregated and desegregated populations in ways that reflect our innermost values and beliefs. From the eugenics theory and movement of the early 1930s to Jensen's support of racial and genetic inferiority, to Hernstein and Murray's powerful findings in *The Bell Curve*, achievement tests and their findings have raised more questions than they appear to solve. Our forefathers left us with tests that even today repeat their inherent biases. Whether these biases are accepted overtly or covertly, considered to be politically correct or incorrect, the fact remains that our current reservoir of academic tests are glaringly biased. Therefore, we submit, findings based on these tests should not be the sole determining factor for admissions into college, advanced placement, or admission into special track programs.

Science and culture can run headlong into collision. Recent results from achievement test results on the FCAT for example, created a furor in Florida. It was found that many minority students who had GPAs of 3.8 failed the FCAT, raising questions about the validity of the FCAT for non-English-speaking Hispanics, and for black students. Other tests, such as the TAAS, that boast increased test scores for Hispanics and other minorities are misused. For example, the materials of the TAAS (the Texas Assessment of Academic Skills) are actually taught to students; as a result, important academic skills are ignored. Teaching tests is a dangerous precedent; it does not serve true academic excellence, because it fails to take into account basic knowledge necessary for elementary, middle, and high school. For example, if geometry has a loading of 1 percent in a test for example, it will not get the same attention and academic classroom focus as would another mathematical concept that had a much higher weighting. We may successfully teach the test, but lose the education. For example, The National Assessment of Educational Progress found in a national study of over 275,000 students in eleven thousand schools tested between January to March 2002 that twelfth graders did poorly in essay and letter writing, a format not usually used in achievement tests. Unfortunately, school funding, resources, and recognition are tied to proving that minority children are doing better. This begs the question: Are we assessing actual achievement?

There are three factors that are startling in their consistency irrespective of state or race. These factors are the school district a child belongs to, the level of parental income, and the enrichment of curricula. Samuel Meyers, Jr., found in a study that African American students were concentrated in schools that ranked 4.5 times poorer in mathematics and two times lower in reading. Second, it is no secret that the higher the family income, the higher the child's SAT score. In fact, Peter Sacks concludes that for every ten-thousand-dollar increase in family income, SAT scores increase by about thirty points. It is no surprise, then that Hispanics who complete their GED and attend college tend to work harder, live healthier lives, and earn more, move to better neighborhoods to improve the education of their children. Thus, school districts with better resources, better teacher education, better teacher-student classroom ratios, and better special-track programs are the key to improved SAT scores and improved education quality for our children. The key is not spending money on school trips and transportation but allocating monies in the budget to basic education and teacher pay. Can we provide the same to our lower income, less educated parents? Surely we can, provided we are willing not only to fund basic education but also equitably disburse funds that are available and teach enriched curricula to improve the ranking of our low-income-district schools. Academic poverty has no place in the schools of a country as wealthy as ours.

An insidious and pervasive factor in poor academic performance is the ambivalence, disillusionment, and confusion seen in the black and Hispanic children. Steele finds that if black children are told a test will evaluate how well they can solve verbal problems, they do as well as their white counterparts. Self-esteem, performance, and racial expectations are closely tied to one another. The one sure way of tackling this problem is to work from preschool up, so children can demonstrate success from a very early age. While many white children attend preschool, many Hispanics do not go to school until kindergarten—a handicap for school-aged children from this minority group at the very outset. Social policy and community leaders need to provide very early access to cognitive development for minority children via Head Start and other early childhood programs. Hispanics in leadership positions need to be more active in connecting young children with a sense of success. Instead of racial vulnerability to failure, there should be a racial thrust to success. As Hillary Clinton has written, it takes a village—a society—to raise a child. With better education, these children have the same potential for success as whites. Thus, affirmative action has an important role in our society, to undo the inbuilt biases in college selection. Colleges and universities should also be required to develop achievement tests that represent actual academic materials, rather than complicated questions that require understanding specific to the dominant white culture.

Social and public policy decisions shape how we teach our children. From Fordham University's complex work on student ambivalence toward success, Steele's finding of stereotypic vulnerability, Hernstein's and Murray's work, and the inequitable representation of minorities in developing normative samples for tests, it appears that what is required is change not only in the way we test our children but also in the way we approach our children in the twenty-first century. Every high school should be required to offer a "gifted and talented" track. Oversized classrooms in overcrowded schools cannot provide this. Talented children bow to peer pressure and conform, thereby giving up their talents in order to fit in and be mediocre. Teachers lose hope and burn out. A gifted-and-talented track will not only attract better teachers but give hope to minority children, who will see success is possible. We suggest that volunteers, such as retired people, develop a "school corps" where they give their time in the cafeteria, library, tutoring, janitorial services, before and after school child care, etc. In that way school districts, instead of outsourcing their needs as they are otherwise forced to do in a depressed economy, could use talent locally available. An oversight committee consisting multi-ethnic representatives of a variety of -professions could be charged with finding creative solutions to a district's educational and administrative problems.

Successful school districts all have gifted-and-talented tracks, and students see their successes, but the majority of students in these tracks are whites and Asians. Ronald Ferguson and his colleagues find that black students are discouraged from taking on more challenging courses. Across the country, the indications are that non-Asian minorities are discouraged from applying for the gifted and talented programs. Schools that are predominantly minority enrolled should fight this trend. Some school districts have realized this need but provide separate schools for their gifted children. This is a form of segregation, the academic isolation of the best students. Instead, the program should be within the actual school system, so that students in it can interact with others, demonstrate the advantages of success, help others resist the pull of mediocrity, act as mentors for younger peers, and be role models to their younger peers. The Tri-State study completed in 2000, proved that enhancing curricula and challenging children from minority, disadvantaged families improved their test scores. Imagine how a gifted-and-talented track that continued the trend could improve SAT scores and eligibility for entrance into our most prestigious colleges. The Associated Press reports findings from National Assessment of Educational Progress data (January to March 2002) in which twelfth graders did very poorly on an essay-writing test that reflected creativity and letter-writing skills—validating the opinion of Gaston Caperton, chair of the College Board for the SAT, that high schoolers need to learn how to write. Only 51 percent of our twelfth graders can write at a basic level. The SAT will have require essay writing in 2005.

Who are the new tests given to? As one AP high honors student said, "My class is the guinea pig for all these new and fancy tests." Instead, test developers need to address different races and socioeconomic levels equally, not proportionally, during the development of normative data in order to eliminate test bias. For example, if a group represents only 5 percent of a population, it does not follow that 5 percent of the sample pool should represent that minority.

Parents are critical in boosting children's self-esteem and eliminating ambivalence toward success—in terms of the active involvement, good listening skills, better communication, positive role modeling, concern for the child's welfare, involvement in activities, recognizing the consequences of parental separation and divorce on the child's well-being, closeness of mother-daughter and father-child bonds, forestalling mediocrity, and instilling dignity and pride in belonging to their minority group. Schools that teach diversity and intercultural acceptance as practical values are likely to produce students who are more accepting of minority students, especially blacks and Hispanics. With every subsequent generation of students, this multicultural ethic is likely to overcome the geographical biases that parents hand over to their children. Another method is to group students within a multicultural format to do research, and learn and argue about other cultural groups' values and belief systems. Greater understanding of another culture will lead to less fear or rejection of other cultures, and less chances of rejection at the higher academic levels.

The cognitive and emotional development of any child starts prior to birth. Prenatal care of the mother is perhaps the most critical factor within minority health practice. Education, frequent home visits to expectant mothers, and programs geared to supporting mothers are most likely lead to the birth of healthy children. We applaud the state of Indiana for providing health care access for every child, but from a social policy point of view, the success of our minority children starts from the health of their mothers. Young teenage mothers should be assisted extensively in continuing with their education or getting GEDs during their pregnancy. Time and again, results have shown a positive correlation between education and health of a mother, and a child's academic success.

From the public policy point of view, the bottom line is educational opportunity for low-income, poorly educated parents, and parenting training, teacher education opportunities, and enriched curricula for our minority students. Jobs that increase parental income following this education will be necessary. Funding will be required to provide resources and rewards, such as vouchers for free child care, food, clothing, assisted housing, and so on. Successful members of minorities can provide some of the training and exposure to business opportunities. Most of these services will need to be voluntary, as resources can be stretched thin by the basic education needs of minority students. As rewards, minorities who provide these opportunities could receive public recognition.

From the psychological point of view, the tests themselves need to be overhauled. Twenty-first century America will require tests that are fully representative of and applicable to all Americans, especially African Americans and Hispanics.

—Kalyani Gopal, Ph.D., HSPP
Licensed clinical psychologist and founding fellow of
the American Board of Advanced Practice Psychologists

INDEX

peanuts, 95

poor: healthcare, 46, 52; nutrition, 29, schools, 46

positive: models, 31; rewards, 69; vs. negative families, 72

poverty, 34

Powell, General Colin, 96

practical set, 47

problem solving, 74, 91, 105

proverbs, learning, 92

quality time, 71

quantifiable scores, 20

racial bias, 38

racially sensitive tests, 39

Ramirez, Marcy, xviii

Ramoli, H. J. A., Dr., xvii

relaxation classes, 12

reliability, 20, 83

Rio Grande, 97

roots, 95

rote memorization, 3

S.O.B., 39, 93, 94

Sacks, Peter, 122

Santana, Carlos, 96

SAT (Scholastic Aptitude Test), 39, 41, 46

school: funds, 45; readiness testing, 6, 17

self-confidence, 76

self-esteem, 25, 36, 61

single parents, 25, 45

Smits, Jimmy, 96

socioeconomic status, 48

Spencer, Tom and Kathy, xviii

standardized tests, vii, viii, xiv, xviii 1, 21, 45, 46

Stanford-Binet Intelligence Scale, 19

Steffey, Susan, xviii

Stowe, Harriet Beecher, 94

subjectivity, xi

substance abuse, 28, 30, 31, 46, 52

TAAS (Texas Assessment of Academic Skills), 122

tabula rasa, 53

teachers, overworked, 32

teenage mothers, 27

Terman, L. M., 19

test bias, ii, xii, xiv, xxi, 22, 39, 94, 103

"test wise" characteristic, 11

testing disability, 13

test-score gap, xx, xxi

Timbuktu, 94, 96

Trevino, Lee, 98

Trinidad, Felix, 98

tri-state study, xxii, 124

Tubman, Harriet, 94

Uncle Tom's Cabin, 95

underground railroad, 95

unfamiliarity, 44

unmotivated teachers, 34

unstructured learning, 48

validity, 20

verbal communication, 35

Villa, Pancho, 96

violence, exposure to, 26
Visclosky, Peter, Congressman, xviii
vocational testing, 10

Washington, Booker T., 94
Wechsler, David, 20
welfare, 29

Wilkerson, Ellen, xviii
Williams, Robert L., 5, 39, 93
Winfrey, Oprah, 31, 43
word games, 33, 44, 71

Yeats, William Butler, 81

ABOUT THE AUTHORS

Harry Gunn has a Ph.D. in clinical psychology. He has been a teacher, a therapist, and most of all a diagnostician. As such, he has evaluated airline hijackers, death-row inmates, business executives, police officers, and firefighters. Dr. Gunn studied at Beloit College, Purdue University, University of Chicago, and Loyola University in Chicago, where he earned his doctorate. His area of research includes the analysis and measurement of problem-solving ability and the development of creative approaches for setting and reaching goals. In 1971 he copublished a study on "Bender Gestalt Performance Among Culturally Disadvantaged Children." This prompted his testing of children from the Appalachian Mountain region.

Dr. Gunn has published numerous books, including *The Test for Success Book; Fear of Success and Guilt over Success; The Test Yourself Book; Manipulation by Guilt; Perceptual and Motor Skill;* and *Investment Euphoria and Money Madness.* Dr. Gunn has also been a newspaper columnist, focusing on providing quick responses to the average person's problems; his expertise was addressing issues pertaining to children and their school performance. He was also a consultant to the Grammar School District in Illinois, where his primary responsibilities included helping students learn how to take tests better, how to build self-esteem, how to become leaders, how to improve concentration, how to make learning fun, how to individualize the learning environment, and how to help children and teens communicate more effectively.

Dr. Gunn has addressed large gatherings, such as the Working Women's Expo. He has taught junior college classes for eleven years, primarily to minority students in Harvey, Illinois. Dr. Gunn is well known for lectures to attorneys and allied professionals. Dr. Gunn has also conducted several seminars on the topic of "Who Moved My Cheese." Additionally, a franchise company—Colonel Sanders Kentucky Fried Chicken—hired him to develop and conduct research to determine the predictability of a franchisee's success based on test data. This includes.

Dr. Gunn is a member of the American Psychological Association, the Illinois Psychological Association, and the American Board of Professional Disability Consultants. Dr. Gunn was appointed by the governor of Illinois to the licensing board for a five-year term. He is an active golfer, scuba diver, and enjoys reading and writing.

Jaswinder Singh has a Ph.D. in clinical psychology. His area of expertise was neuropsychological assessment of cognitively disadvantaged individuals. He completed his postdoctoral training at the University of California at Davis and Berkeley, and at Northwestern University. He has been actively involved in the design and use of tests to measure various cognitive abilities of adults and children. He served as an adjunct assistant professor of psychiatry and behavioral sciences in the Department of Psychiatry at Northwestern University in Chicago. He also served on the staff at the University of Chicago.

Dr. Singh's publishing history includes a recent book, *Americanization of New Immigrants: People Who Come to America and What They Need to Know*, published through University Press of America, as well as numerous journal articles. In response to the tragedy of 9/11 he wrote *America on Fire: A Poetic Tribute to the Memories of 9-11-2001* (published through Cameo Publications), documenting the emotional trauma of the victims' families. He is also the coauthor of *Between the Pages*. He has given many invited lectures to lay audiences as well as the scientific community on this and related topics.

Dr. Singh has done radio and television interviews and is routinely interviewed by newspapers and print columnists. He has a strong publication record in the field of neuropsychology. Dr. Singh received a Young Investigator Award in 1994 from the National Alliance of Research in Schizophrenia and Depression (NARSAD) to conduct research in assessing cognitive abilities of patients with a variety of neuropsychiatric diseases. As a mental health professional he specializes in dealing with family, children, and adults in crisis and experiencing stress and trauma.

Dr. Singh is an active researcher, practitioner, and writer. Currently, he is the director of psychotherapeutic and counseling services at the Mid-America and Psychological and Counseling Services. He provides diagnostic services to minorities, especially African Americans. Many of the ideas for this current book have stemmed from his nearly twenty years of experience working with African Americans and other minority populations.

Dr. Singh is a member of the American Psychological Association, the Illinois Psychological Association, and the American Board of Professional Disability Consultants. He is diplomate of the American Board of Psychological Specialties, a Certified Psychologist, a Licensed Clinical Professional Counselor, and a Licensed Mental Health Counselor in the states of Indiana and Illinois.